Lucky Dog.

RESCUED
FROM THE STREETS
OF SUGAR HILL, NORTH GEORGIA

A Note from the Photographer

Our world has become sanitized of dogs. Most of us leave our dogs at home when we have to go out, not because we don't want them with us, but because they simply aren't welcome where we're going.

Imagine a world where you brought your dog to work, to your favorite restaurant, bookstore, or boutique. Imagine enjoying the sunset with your faithful companion, both of you exhausted, a sticky, sand-covered Frisbee in your beach bag.

Imagine '30A,' a twenty-mile stretch of coastal wonderland along Florida's panhandle where dogs are not only welcomed, they are given a place of honor.

When I see dogs lying on the floor in the shops, under the tables in cafes, and joyfully playing on the beach, there is a sense of 'rightness' to the scene. These 'Dogs of 30A' are not just pets; they are full-fledged members of the community, celebrated with their own 'Dog Wall,' 'Yappy Hour,' and now, this book.

I have chosen black and white photography in order to capture the nostalgic feel of these scenes. Blending art with love, each photo was chosen in an attempt to convey what can be possible in a community who dares to dream. The time has come to celebrate this community... a community whose dogs might be the luckiest dogs in the world.

~ TONIA SHATZEL, DVM

Shep

LaGRANGE BAYOU
LOVED BY: TONIA & TURNER SHATZEL & ROB WOOD

"The FIDELITY of a DOG is a precious GIFT demanding no less binding MORAL responsibilities than the FRIENDSHIP of a HUMAN being."

~ Konrad Lorenz

Special Thanks To...

Linda White, at Sundog Books in Seaside, who gave us the courage to produce this book. Along with her trusty old girl, "Patty", Linda inspired us, educated us, and gave us the encouragement we needed to forge ahead.

And To...

Mike and Angela Ragsdale for creating such a strong and welcoming community with the "30A" brand. Thank you for leading the way, and allowing the Dogs of 30A to be your "best friend".

All Our Best,

from the Dogs of 30A team

"Lick!"

"For fourteen years, Patty has come to work every single day in order to greet customers and make them feel at home."

Patty
SUNDOG BOOKS
SEASIDE
LOVED BY: LINDA & BOB WHITE

Bogey
30A.COM
CERULEAN PARK
WATERCOLOR
LOVED BY: THE RAGSDALES

Bailey

SMILING FISH CAFE
GULF PLACE
LOVED BY: RUDY WEBER

Captain Henry Morgan Atchley

THE MASCOT & LOGO FOR THE DOGS OF 30A
LOVED BY: GREG, KERI, ELIZABETH & NATALIE ATCHLEY

Roxy

Grayton Beach
loved by: Melanie, Brad & Meghan Clark

Lulu

GRAYTON BEACH
LOVED BY: THE NELSON FAMILY

Lulu
GRAYTON BEACH
LOVED BY: THE NELSON FAMILY

Sweet Pea
GRAYTON BEACH
LOVED BY: MELANIE, BRAD & MEGHAN CLARK

Maggielee
Blue Mountain Beach
Loved by: Kerrie Beth Dalal & Robert Lee

RESCUED
ADOPTED FROM
ORANGE BEACH, AL

"He's the love of my life."

Copper
SEASIDE ANIMAL RESCUE
SEASIDE
LOVED BY: DANIELLE SNYDER

Ranger
FROSTBITES
SEASIDE
LOVED BY: DANIELLE SNYDER

RESCUED
ADOPTED FROM
PAWS, FT. WALTON

Riley
WATERCOLOR
LOVED BY: THE WHITAKERS

Lucky Dog. 2010   THE DOGS OF 30A

Miss Piggy
Grayton Beach
Loved by: Angie & Chadden Lee Johnston

RESCUED
from Canine Rescue &
Rehabilitation in Santa Rosa Beach

Dewey

Shorty's Surfside & Topside
Grayton Beach
Loved by: Henry Patterson & Karen Sommers

Gris Gris
Sandestin
Loved by: Muki Malec

> "Voodoo has brought the best of times to our family."

Voodoo
Sandestin
Loved by: Nicole & Keith Sharp

Lucky Dog. 2010

"He is our baby, companion and best friend."

Zeke

VAN BUTLER ELEMENTARY
SANTA ROSA BEACH
LOVED BY: SCOTT & CONNIE SHEAR

Gracie

VAN BUTLER ELEMENTARY
SANTA ROSA BEACH
LOVED BY: TINA & DUNCAN

30 THE DOGS OF 30A Lucky Dog. 2010

RESCUED
Adopted from
Alaqua Animal Refuge

Emme

The Thompson Residence
Sandestin
Loved by: Valerie & Mike Thompson

Hurley
Seaside's Ruskin Place Artist Colony
Seaside
Loved by: Calvin Shepard & Suzanne & Tony Lagratta

Truman

GRAYTON BEACH
LOVED BY: THE LAMB FAMILY

RESCUED
Adopted from Chipley Rescue Center

"Obviously, Darla's family was lost in the Amazon Jungle, because why else would such a sweet little dog be left all alone?"

Darla

Santa Rosa Pottery
Santa Rosa Beach
Loved by: Debby Orr

"Belle Bottoms has a quirky love and enigmatic wanderlust that is infectious. To know her is to be loved by her."

Belle Bottoms

ROSEMARY BEACH
LOVED BY: ANNE HUNTER

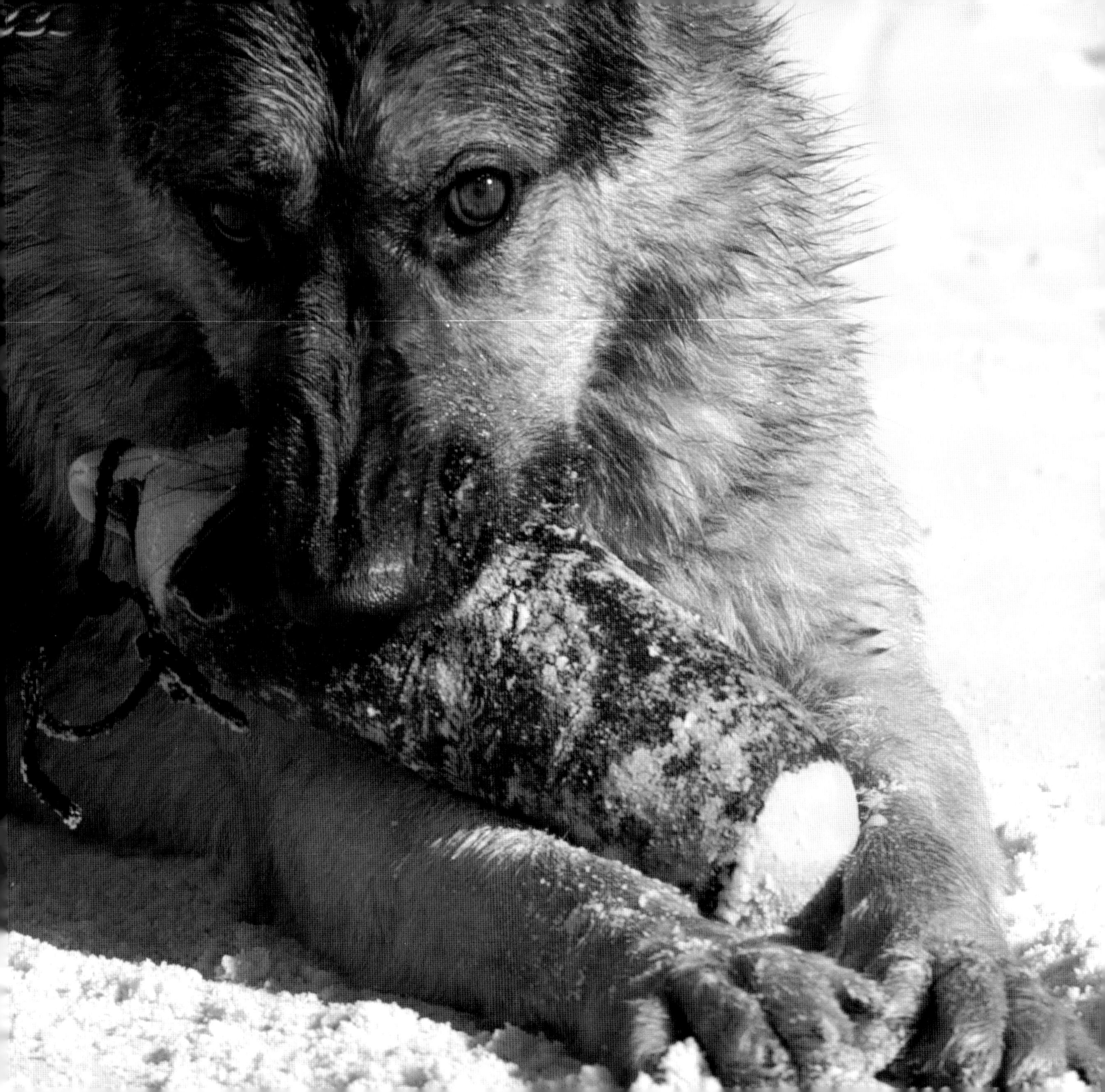

Toccoa
WATERCOLOR
LOVED BY: ED & DONNA MACDONALD

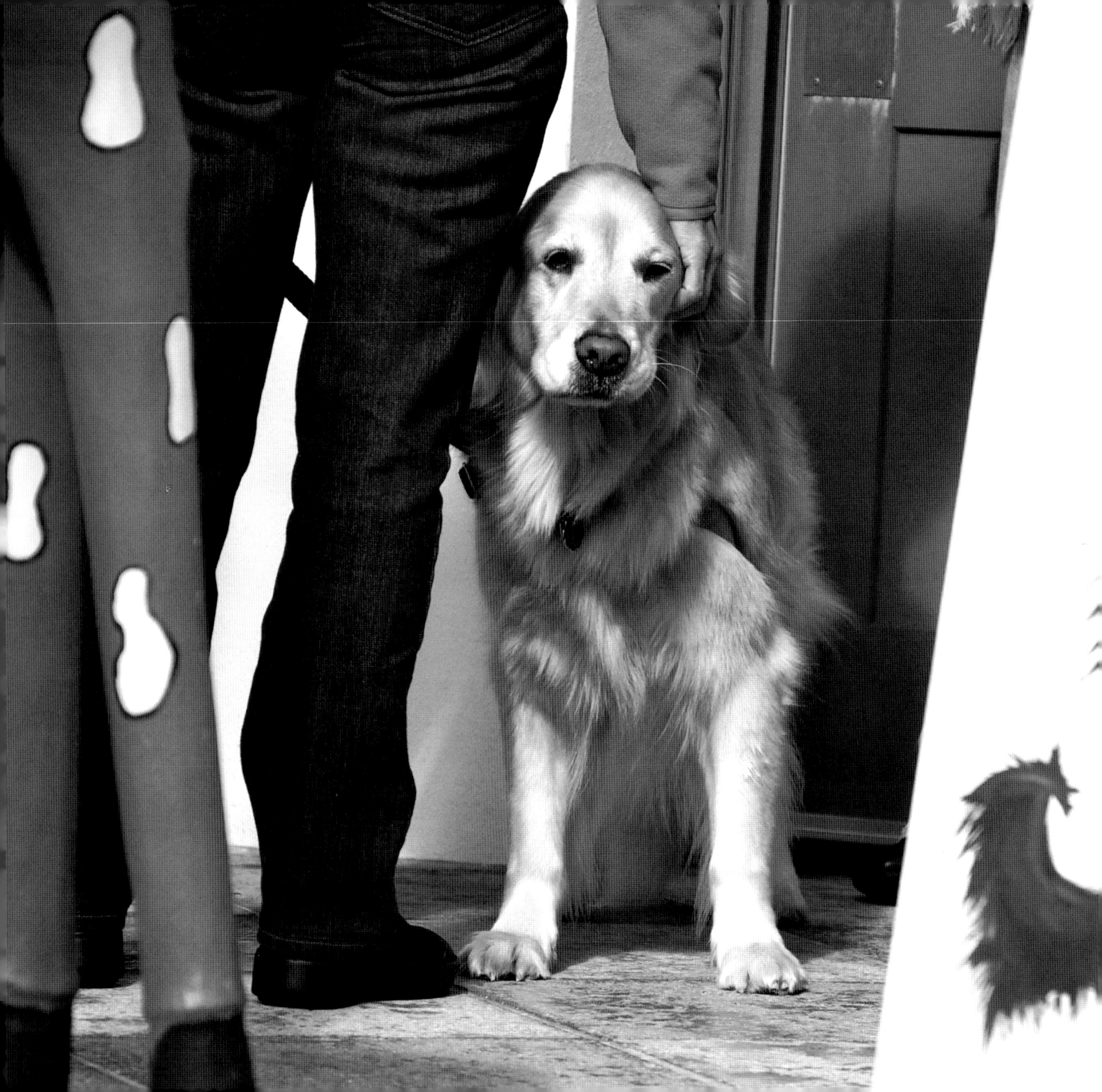

Frannie

THE BLUE GIRAFFE
WATERCOLOR
LOVED BY: NAN & RICK SROUFE

> "Daily 30A travelers often slow down, shouting, 'Hey Frannie!' recognizing her distinctive ploom-of-a-tail sashaying down the bike path."

Emma

THE BLUE GIRAFFE
WATERCOLOR
LOVED BY: NAN & RICK SROUFE

Frannie & Emma

CERULEAN PARK
WATERCOLOR
LOVED BY: NAN & RICK SROUFE

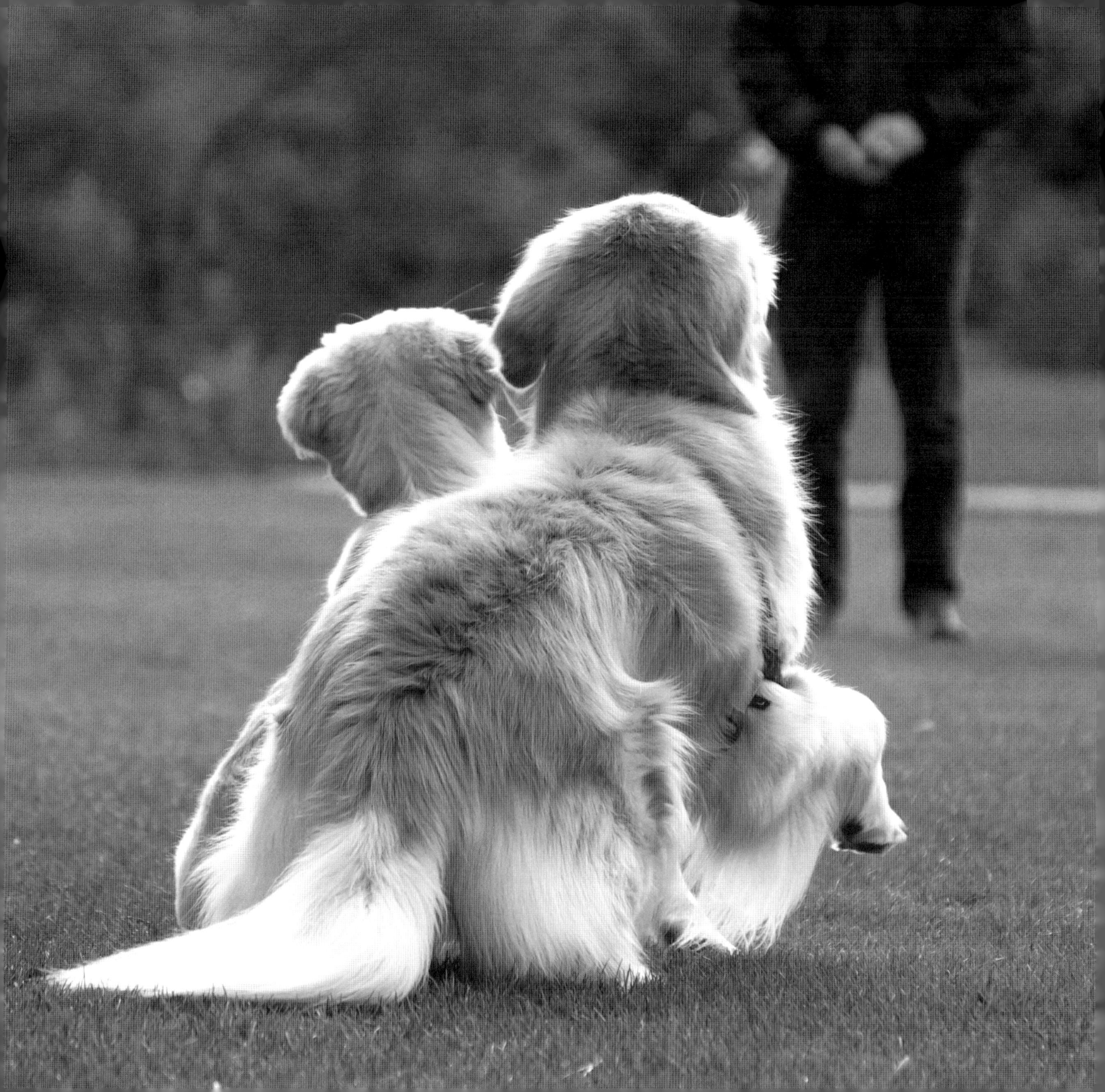

Snickers

SEASIDE'S RUSKIN PLACE ARTIST COLONY
SEASIDE
LOVED BY: JEFF & SHEILA WACHSMAN

Honey

SEASIDE'S RUSKIN PLACE ARTIST COLONY
SEASIDE
LOVED BY: TODD & PAULINE SUTCLIFFE

Retired Racers
ADOPTED FROM THE GREYHOUND PETS OF AMERICA OF THE EMERALD COAST

"A wet dog running on a tile floor is like running on ice. Just before Honey fell, she grazed our end table and went sliding down the hall on her butt. This home inspection was falling apart fast, and my heart sank, thinking Honey might never be ours. As if that weren't bad enough, the Greyhound adoption dog handler ran in with wet shoes, fell, and as she slid by all of us on her butt, hit the table again. That was enough to make the lamp go up in the air, and we watched in horror as it fell to the floor. The sound of the lamp crashing to pieces broke the silence, and everyone in my living room was now looking down, not saying a word. I mustered up the courage to speak. 'Hey, Charlie, this must be the most interesting home visit you have ever been on.' Charlie replied without missing a beat, 'Yep, it's up there, all right. So, when do you want your dog?'"

Snickers

SEASIDE'S RUSKIN PLACE ARTIST COLONY
SEASIDE
LOVED BY: JEFF & SHEILA WACHSMAN

"Snickers and I spend a lot of time walking around Seaside. When people ask if she is a Greyhound and if we rescued her, I always say 'No, she rescued us.'"

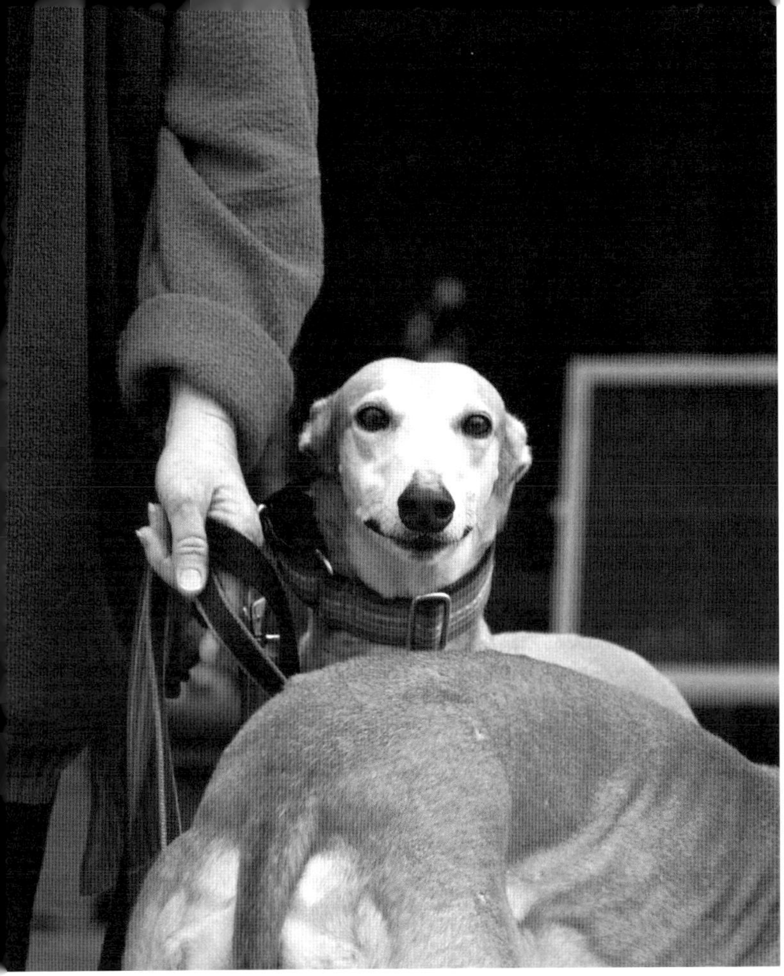
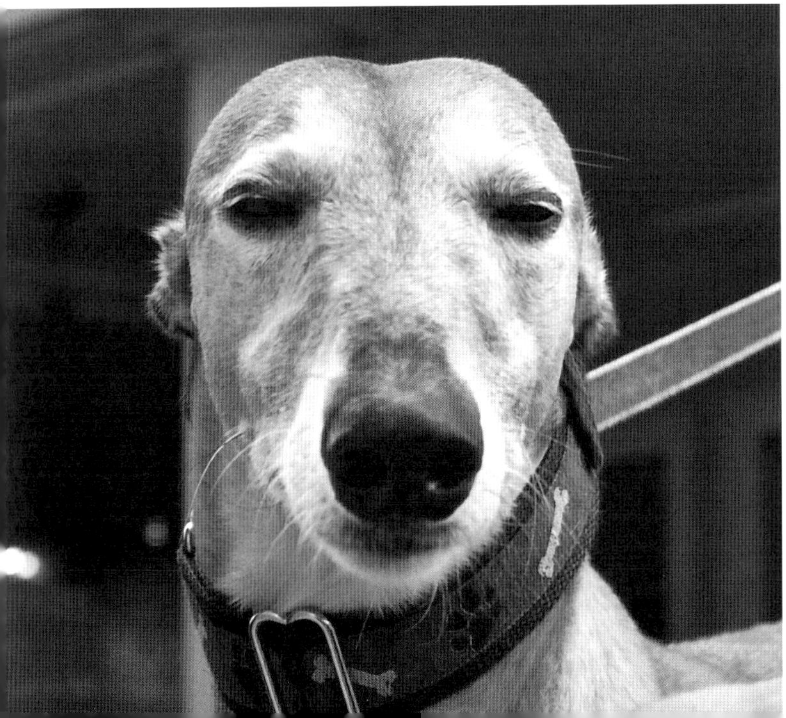
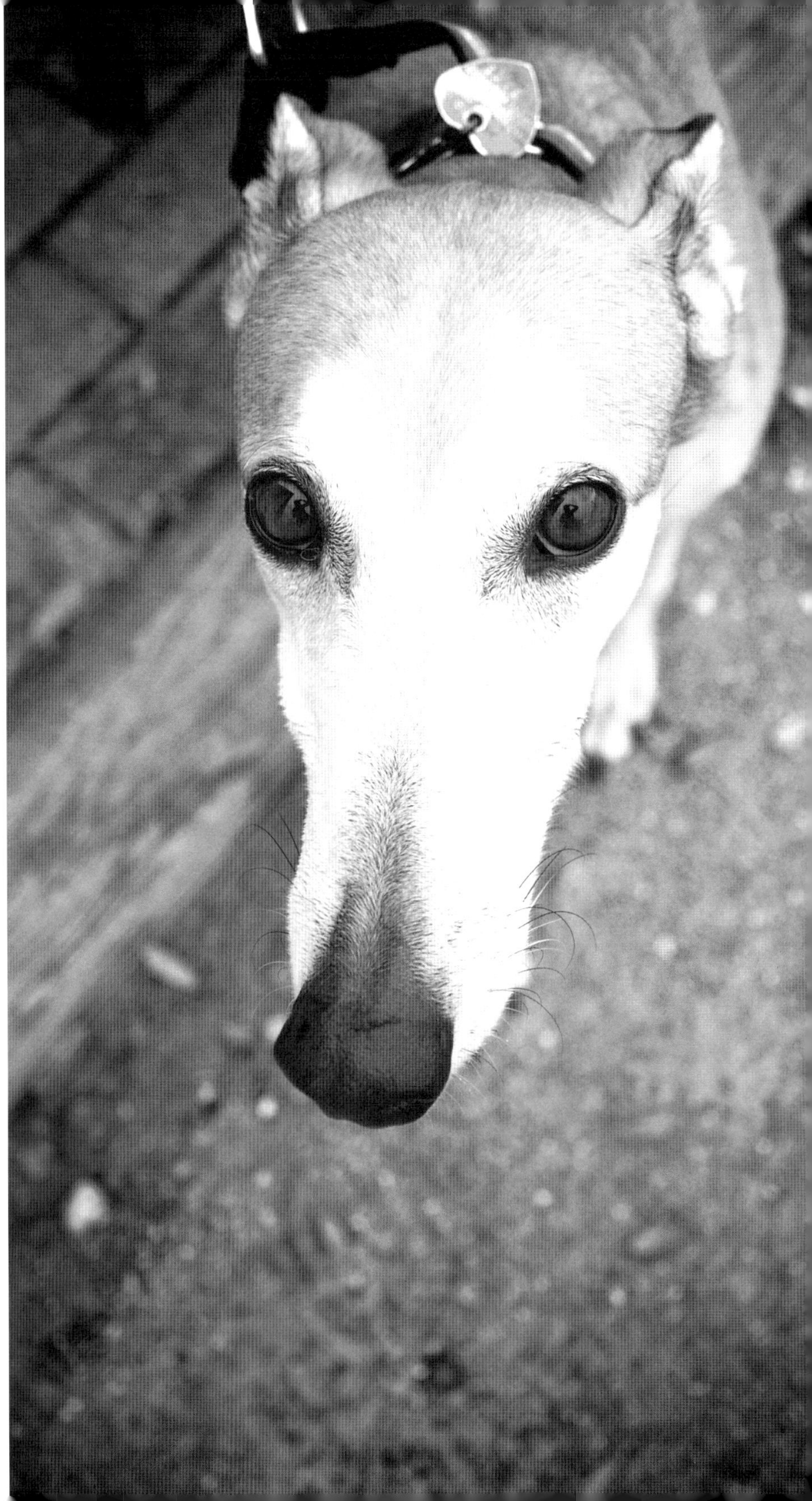

RESCUED
Adopted from
Panhandle Animal Welfare Society
(PAWS), Ft. Walton Beach, Florida

Skyy

Blue Mountain Liquors & Market
Blue Mountain
loved by: Christy Haynes

Madison & Ellie

POINT WASHINGTON
LOVED BY: DENISE EARLES

Bella
SANDESTIN
LOVED BY: THE MOLITERNO FAMILY

Lucky Dog. 2010   THE DOGS OF 30A

Magic, Rosco & Dasher
Seaside
Loved by: Mark, Buffie & Nick Dupuis

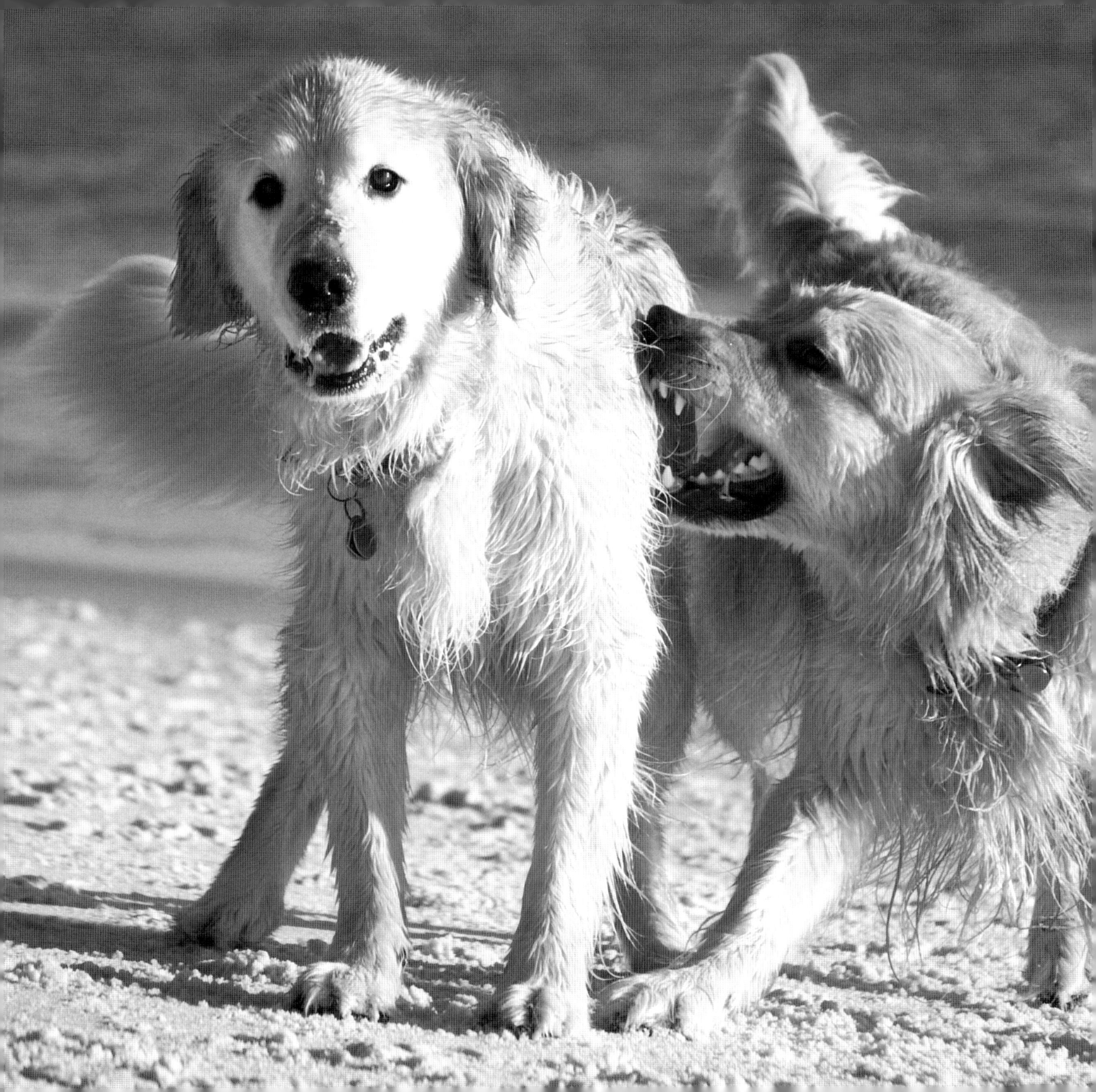

Magic, Rosco & Dasher

SEASIDE

LOVED BY: MARK, BUFFIE & NICK DUPUIS

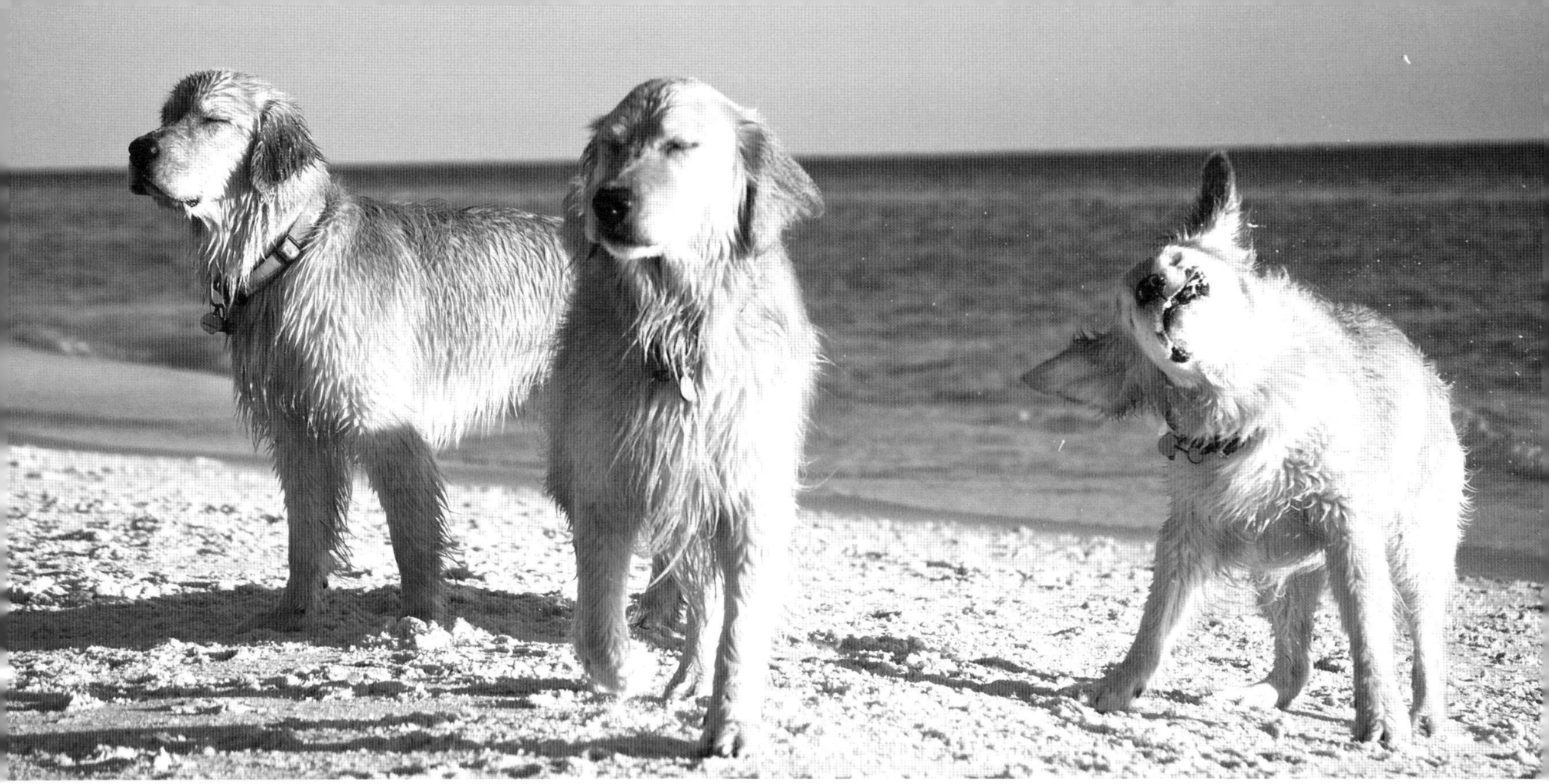

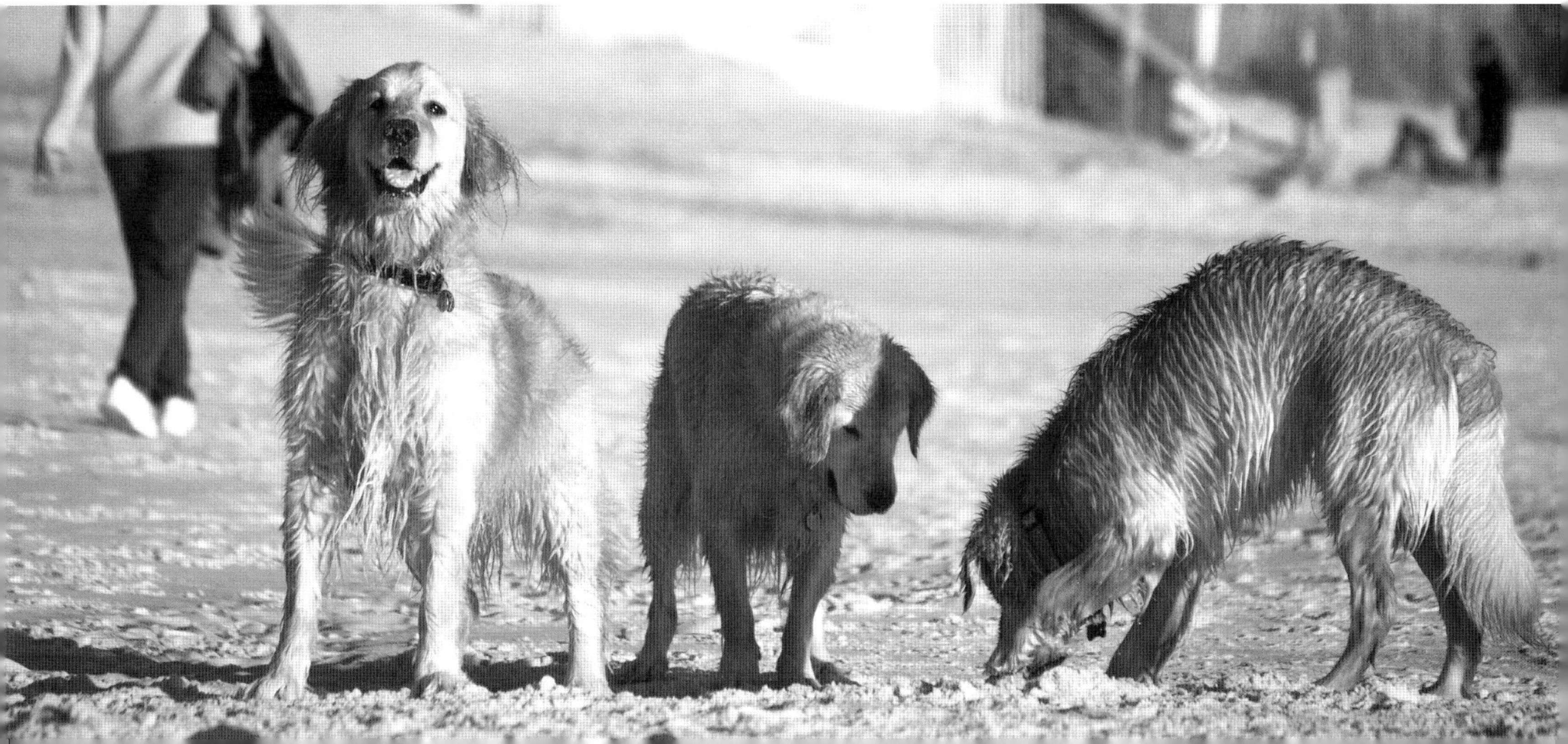

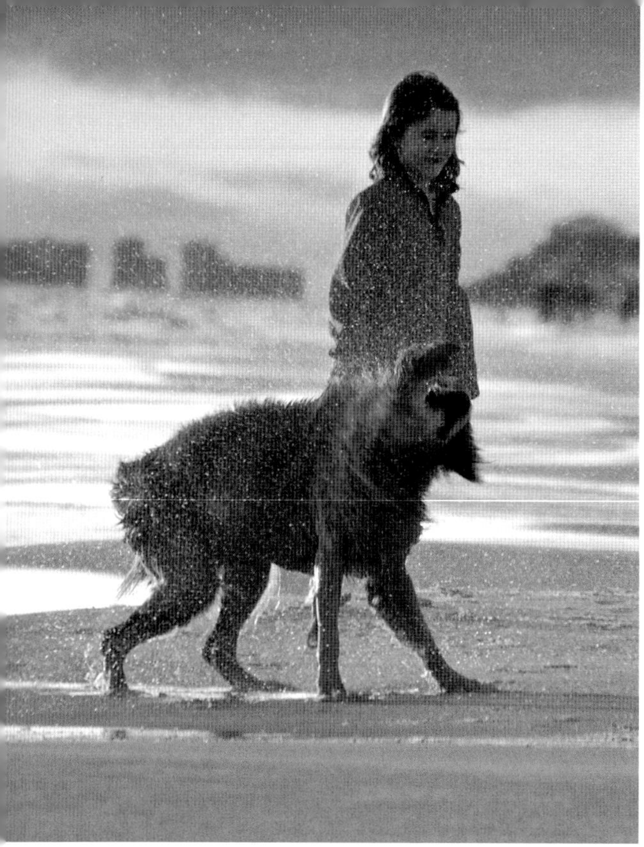
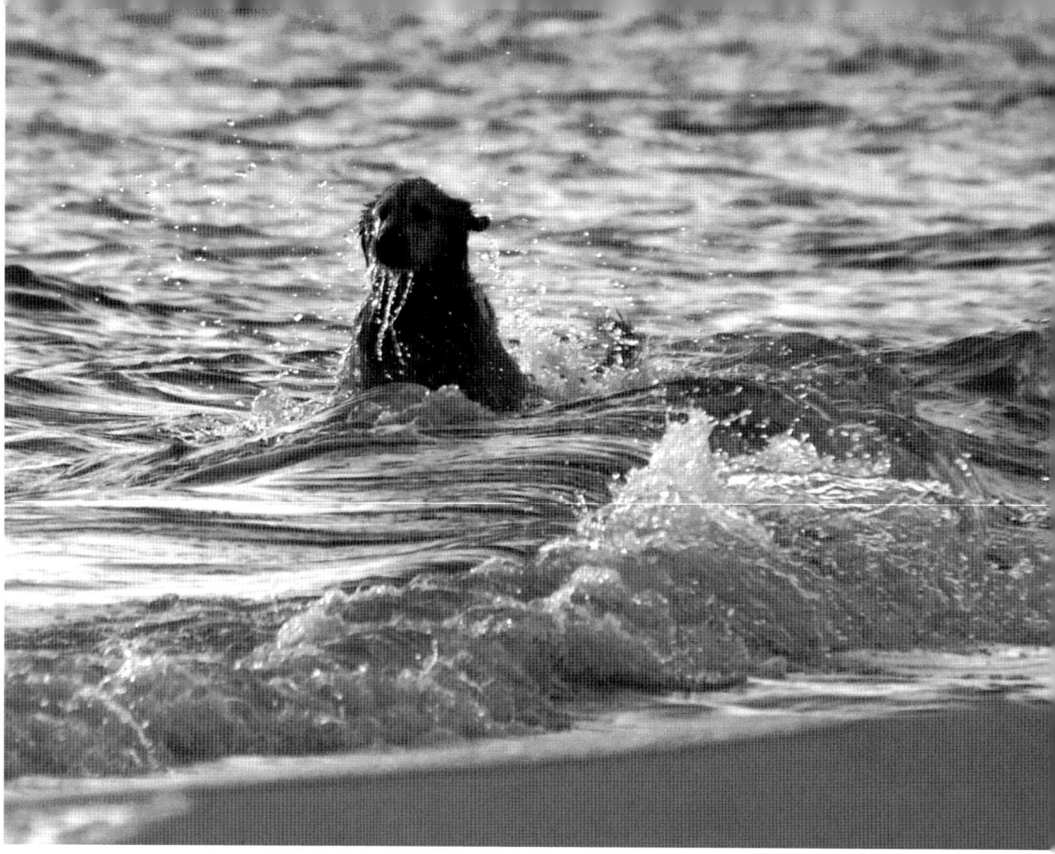
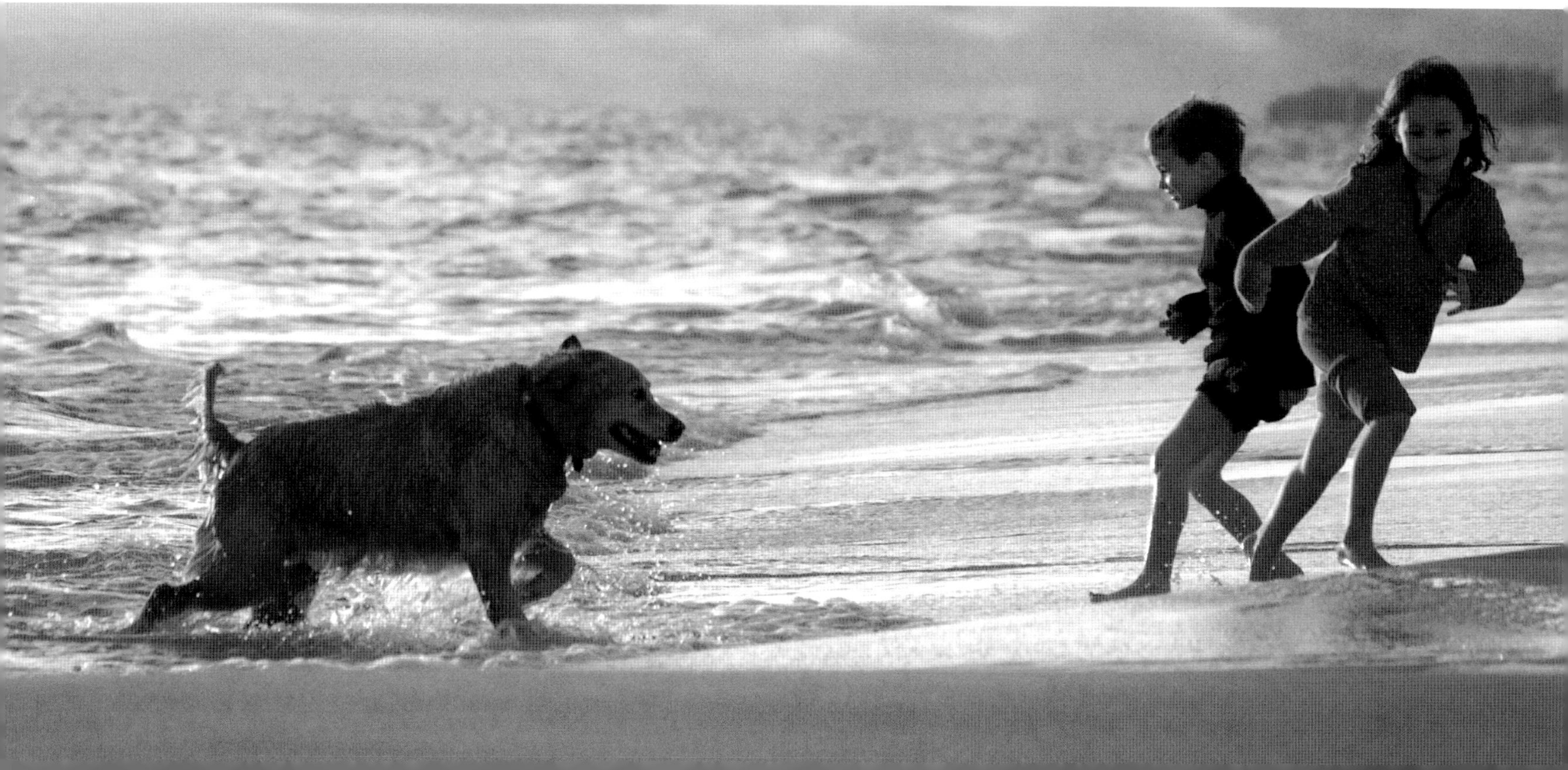

Sophie

SEASIDE

LOVED BY: TERRI & BLAIR SCHMIDT-FELLNER

Vida

SEASIDE

LOVED BY: THE WEAVER FAMILY

Frankie

SEASIDE

LOVED BY: MURIEL GOTTESMAN

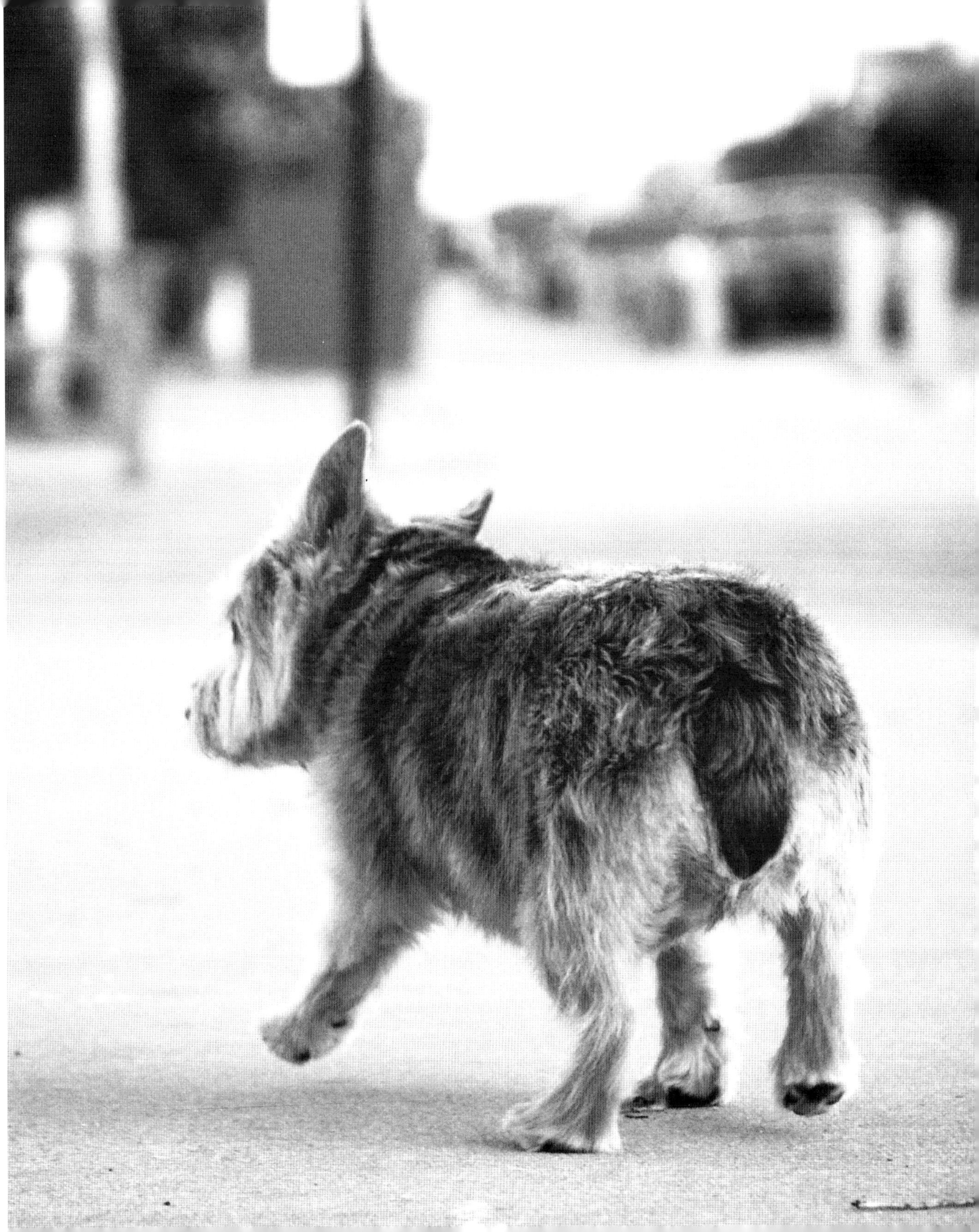

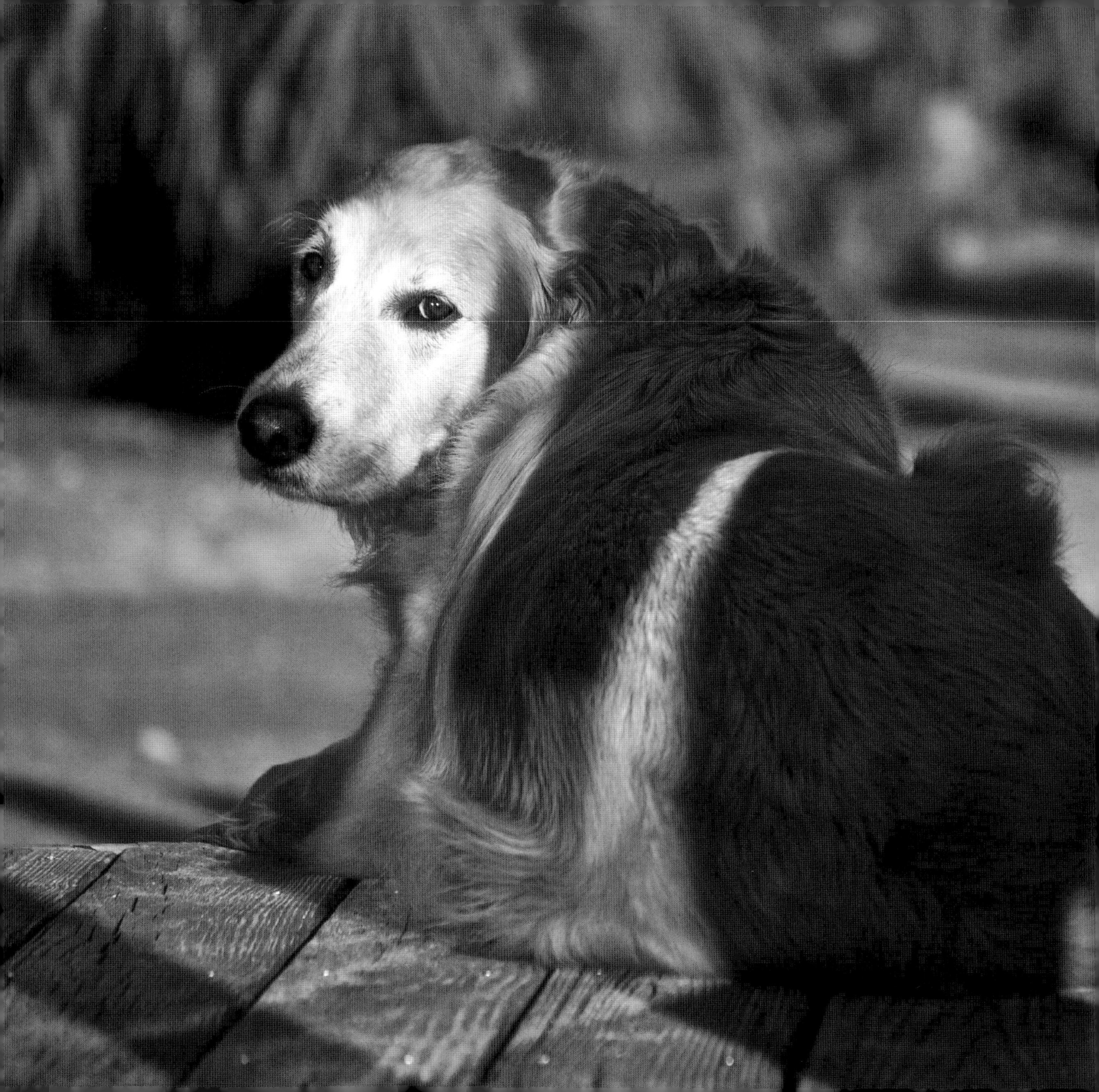

Belle

GYPSEA
GRAYTON BEACH
LOVED BY: THE DOHERTY FAMILY

"When we go to the beach without them, we have to spell 'B E A C H...' but I think they have pretty much caught on to that one now!"

Sera & Beni
BLUE MOUNTAIN BEACH
LOVED BY: JOHNDRA CULP & JILL RICHARDS

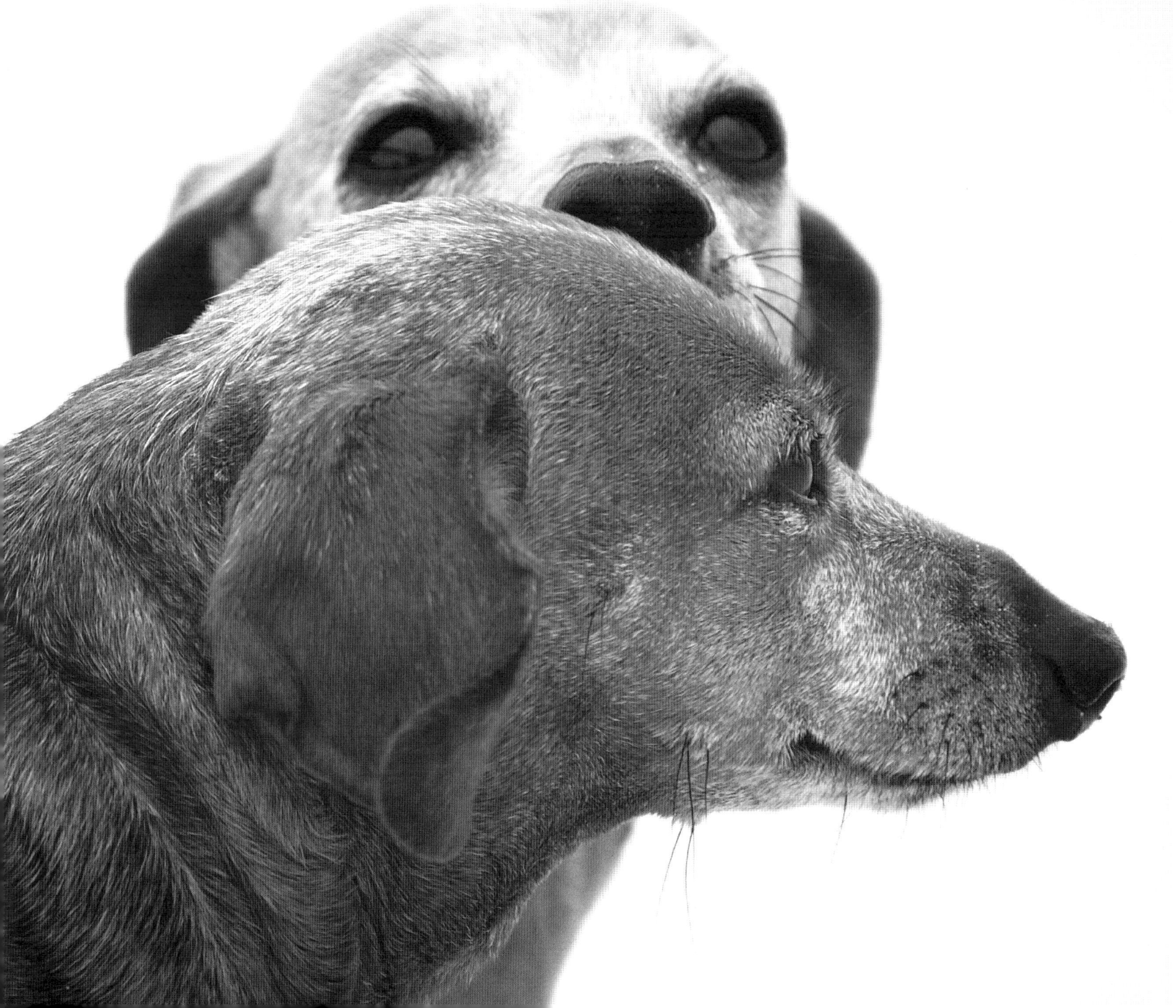

Lucy

YELLOWFIN OCEAN SPORTS
SEAGROVE BEACH
LOVED BY: LYNN SULLIVAN & EVERYONE AT YELLOWFIN OCEAN SPORTS

THE DOGS OF 30A   Lucky Dog. 2010

LIVE BAIT
OPEN
PENN
ST.CRO
OPEN

S.T Fins
$49.95
PADDLEBOY

SPORTSMAN'S BEST: INSHORE FISHING

Lucky Dog. 2010

Ada

SANTA ROSA BEACH
LOVED BY: NANCY & JOE KNIGHT

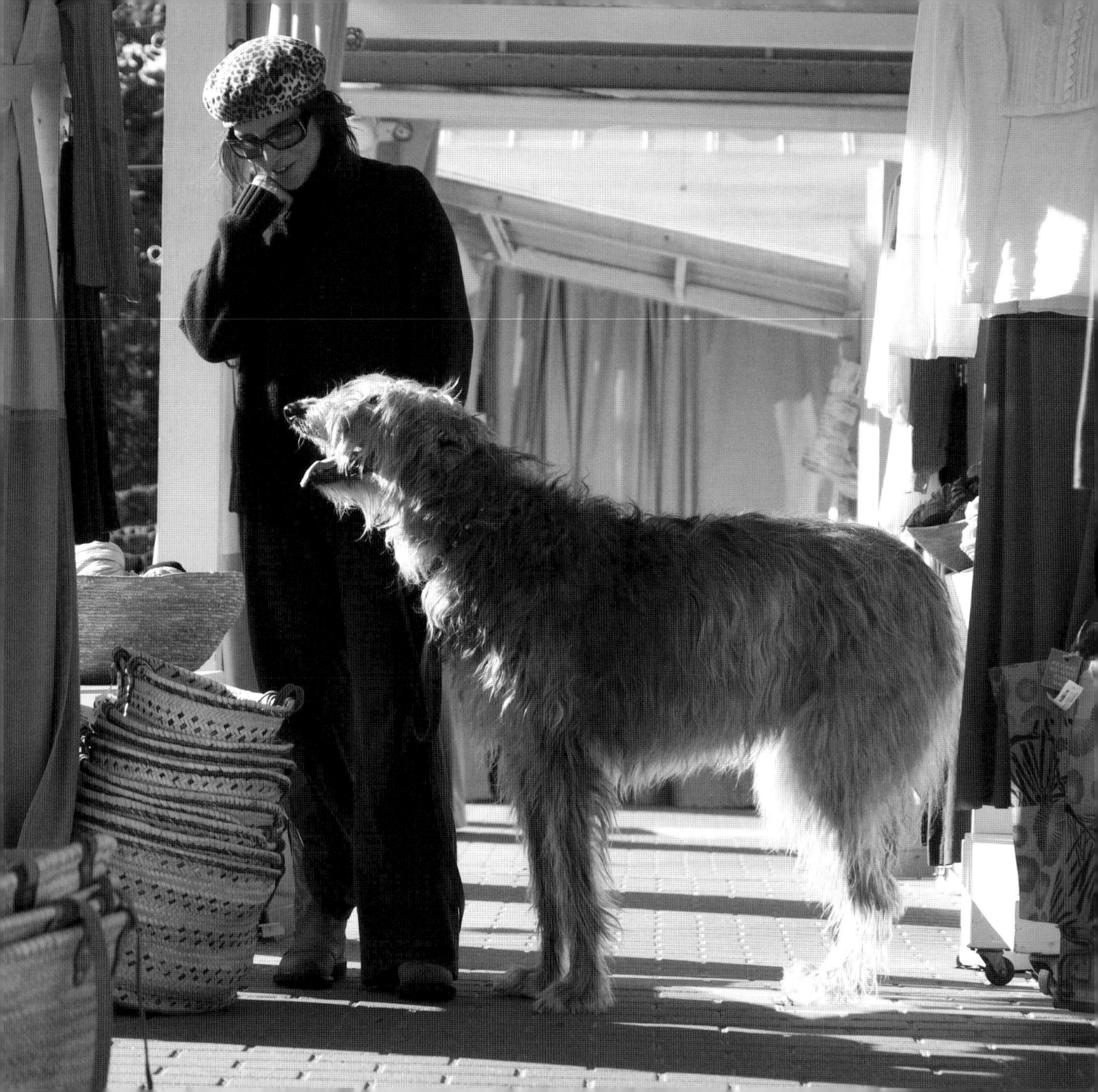

Greta

Perspicasity
Seaside

Loved by: Laney Blanchard

RESCUED
ADOPTED FROM
PIT BULL PROJECT IN SEATTLE

"Adopting Ella was the best decision I have ever made. Seeing what love, patience and hard work can do for a dog from a rough past is an experience I wish everyone could have...and every day I'm rewarded with the unconditional love from Ella. Who could ask for anything more?"

Ella
SEASIDE
LOVED BY: SOFIA PODLUSKY AND JOSEPH MUNOZ

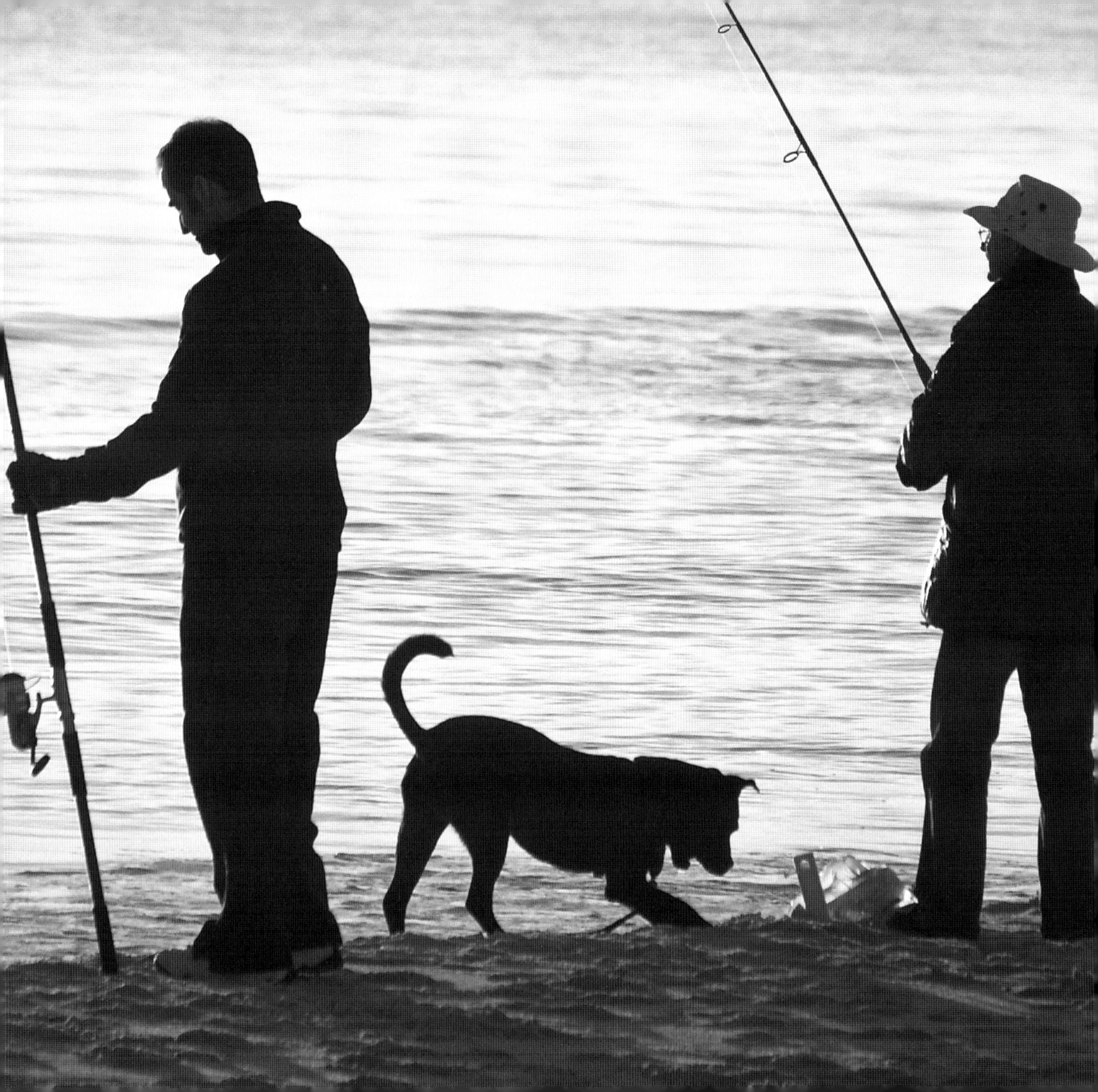

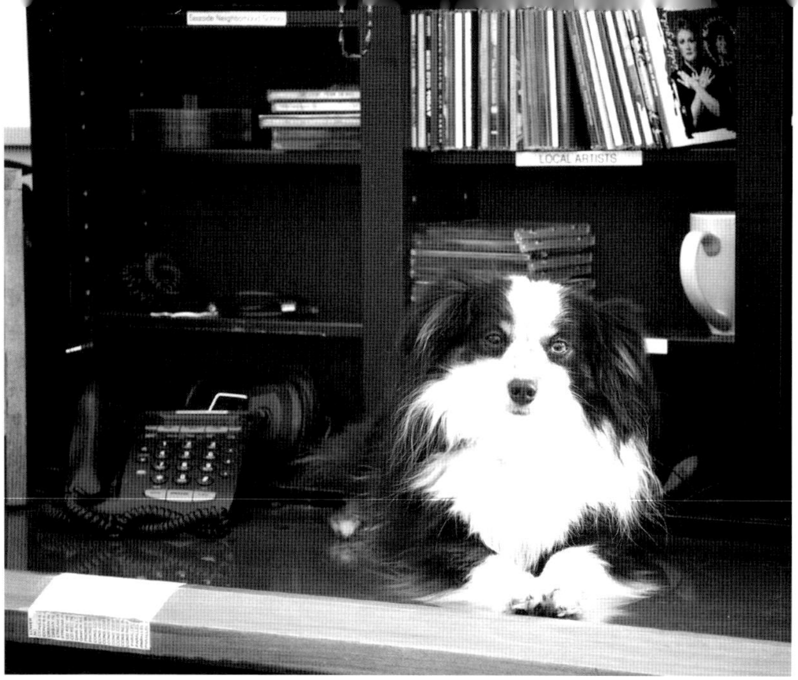
LOCAL ARTISTS

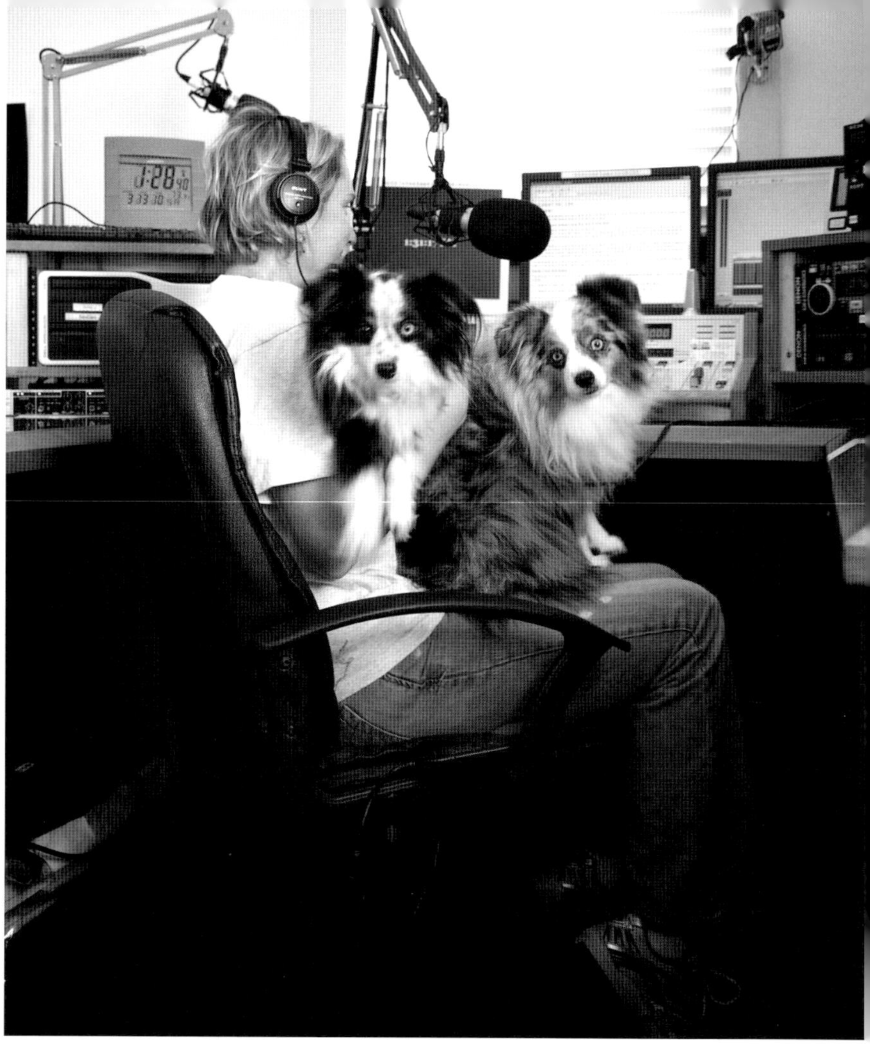

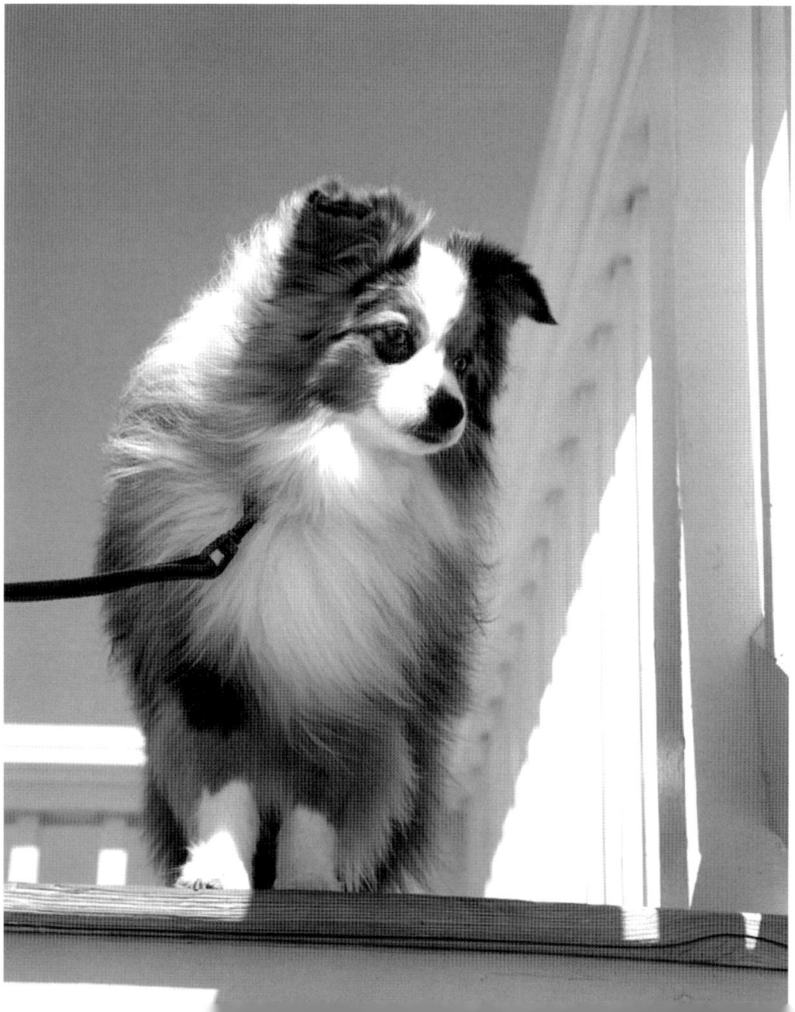

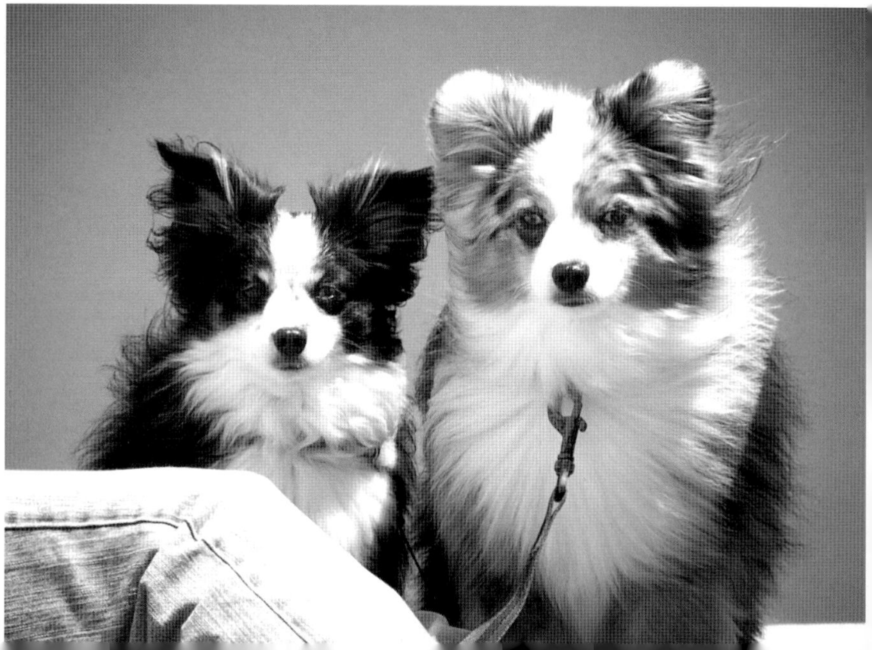

Rocky & Skip
30A Radio Studio
Seaside
Loved by: Leslie Kolovich

Lucky Dog. 2010   THE DOGS OF 30A   71

"He speaks with his eyes."

Marley
CENTRAL SQUARE
SEASIDE
LOVED BY: BILLIE GAFFREY

Izzie

CENTRAL SQUARE
SEASIDE
LOVED BY: ALLISON STRICKLAND

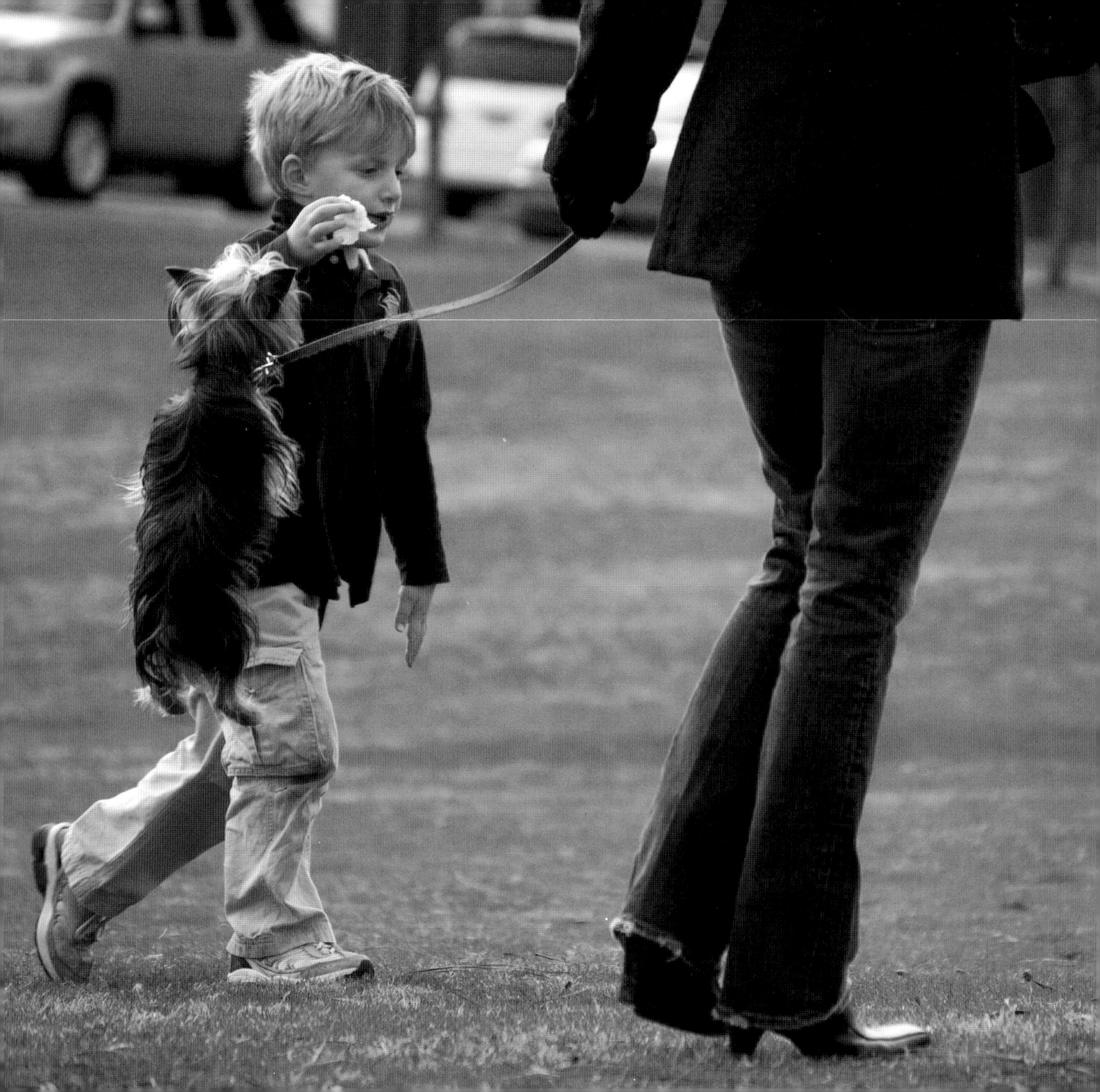

Jake

SEASIDE

LOVED BY: THE GUERNSEY FAMILY

Lucky Dog. 2010

Leo

SEASIDE
LOVED BY: SANDI FISKE, JERRY ANDERSON & JULIE

Ginger

GRAYTON BEACH
LOVED BY: VANESSA KENNEDY

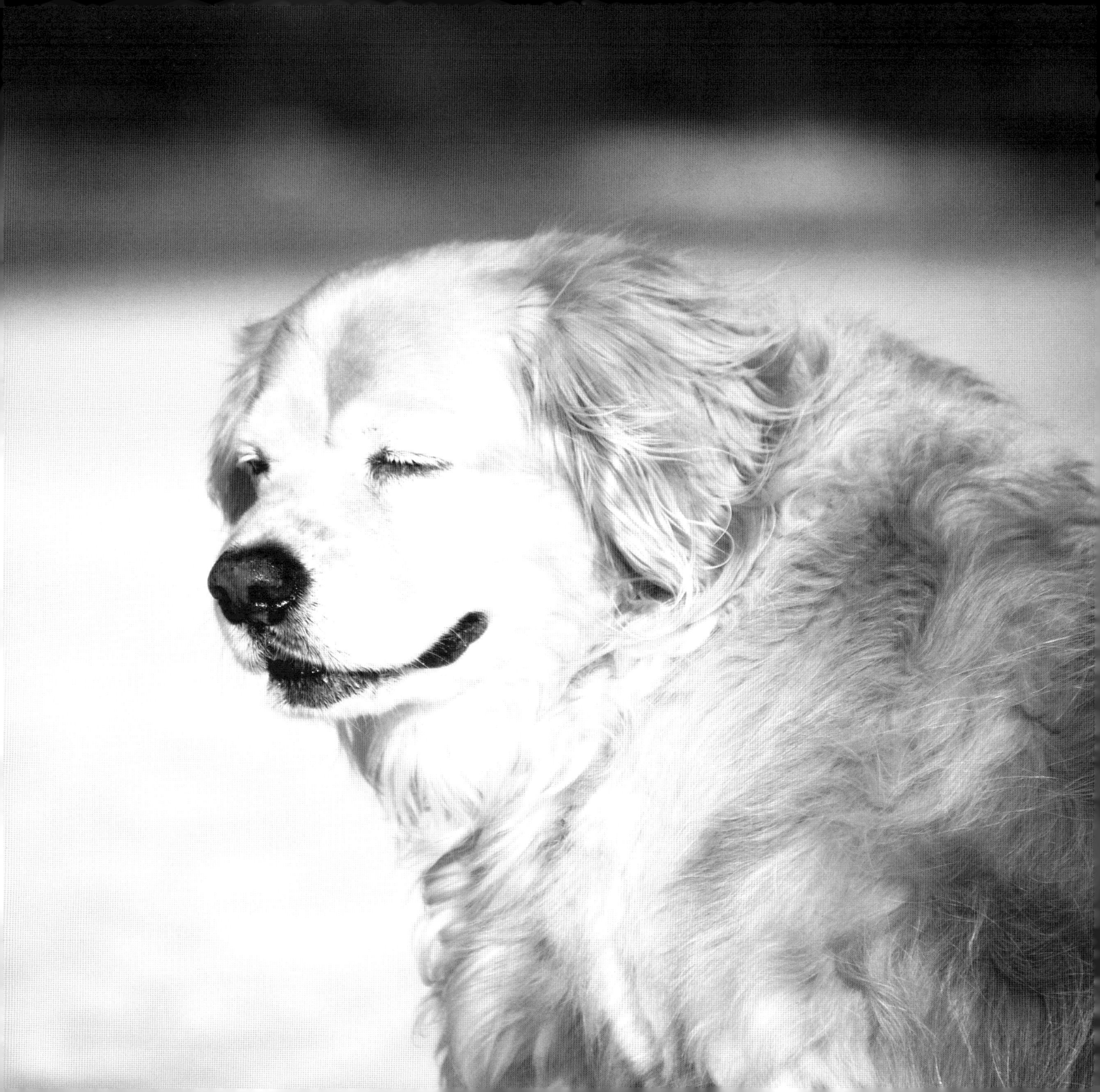

Carly
GRAYTON BEACH
LOVED BY: AL & BARBARA PATISAUL

THE DOGS OF 30A   Lucky Dog. 2010

Winnie
Seaside
Loved by: Bert Trucksess

Steve

GREAT SOUTHERN CAFE
SEASIDE
LOVED BY: DAVE GUTOS

Jasmine

GREAT SOUTHERN CAFE
SEASIDE
LOVED BY: JOHN ORMOND & CHRIS SMITH

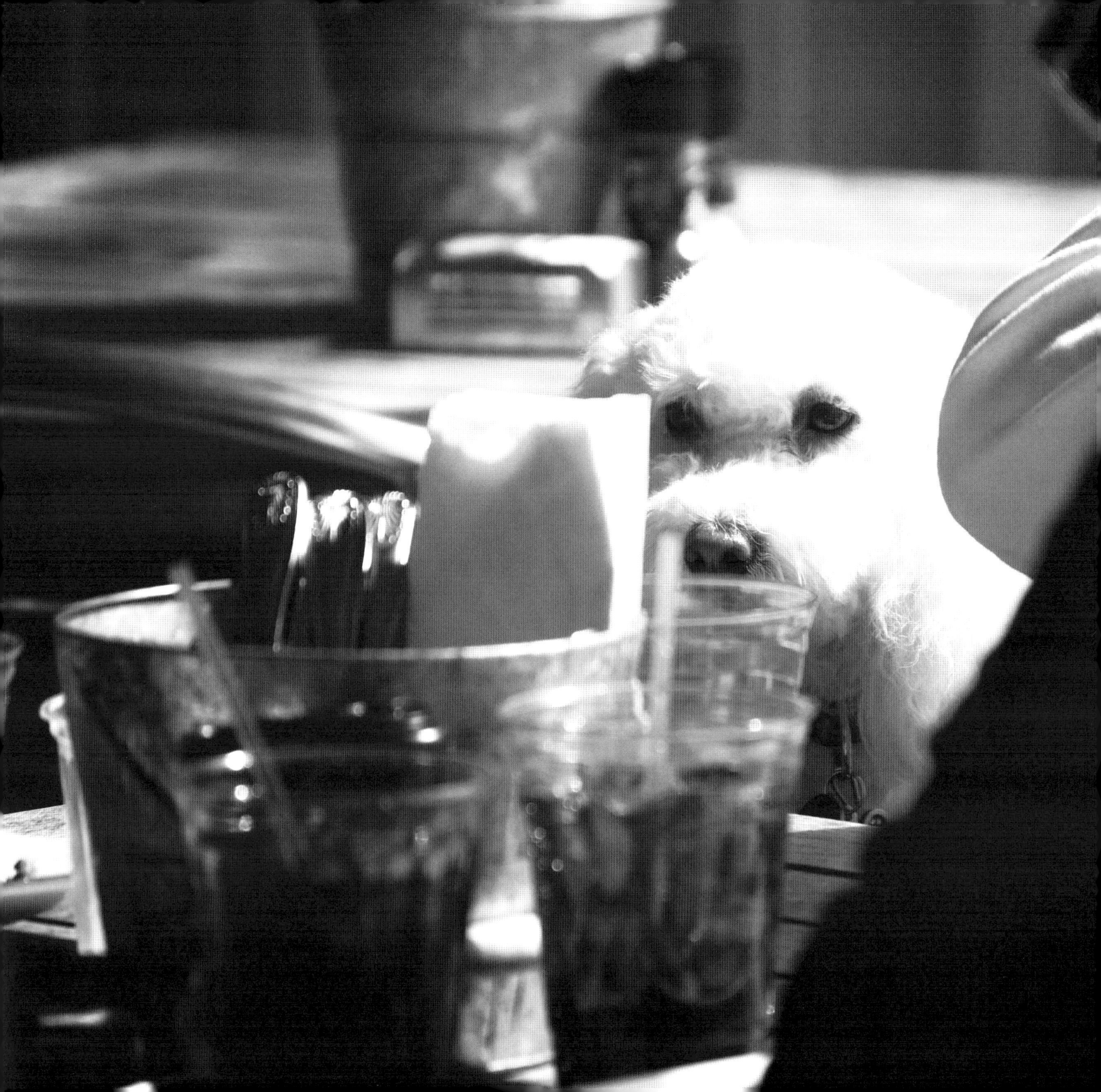

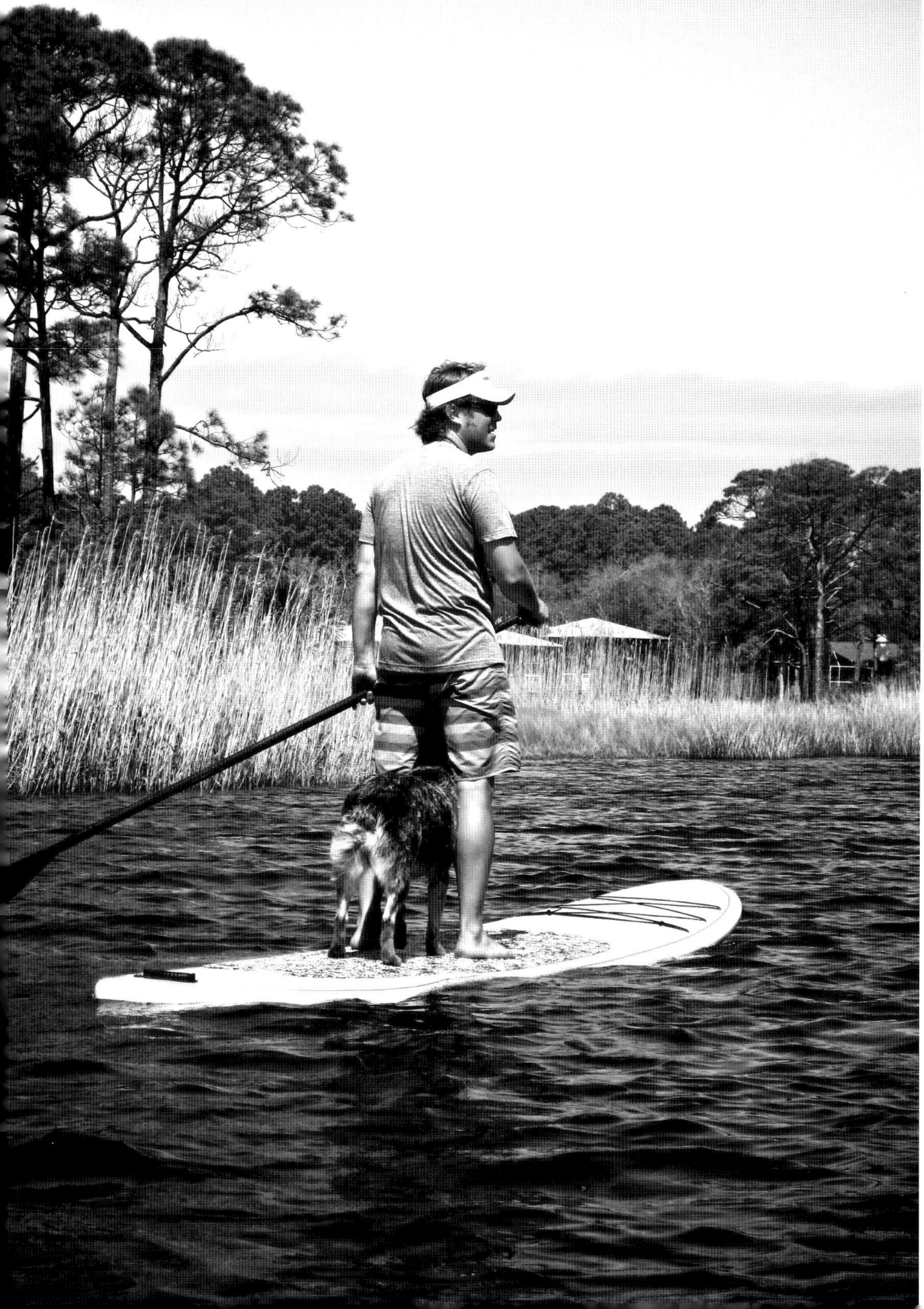

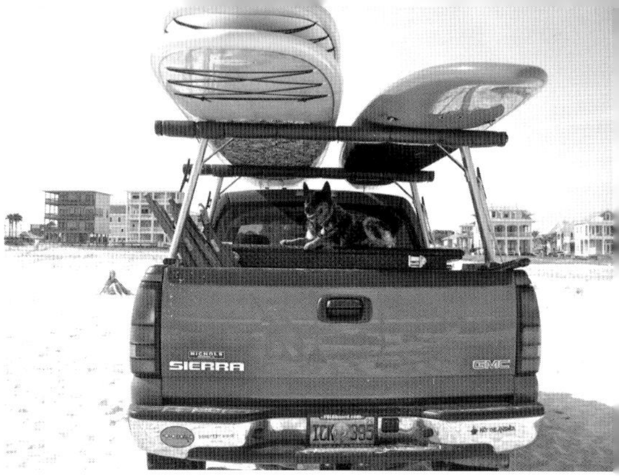
SIERRA

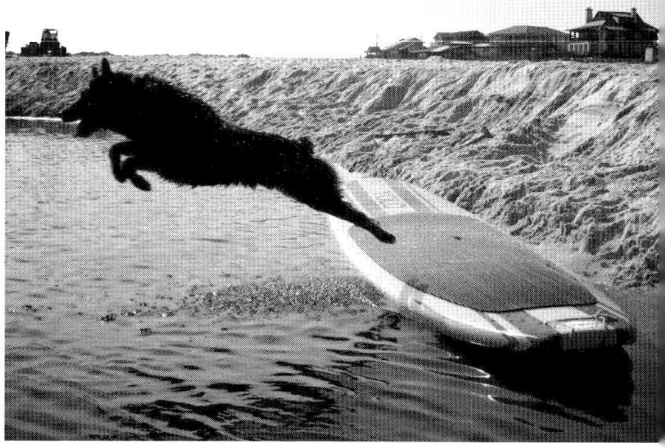

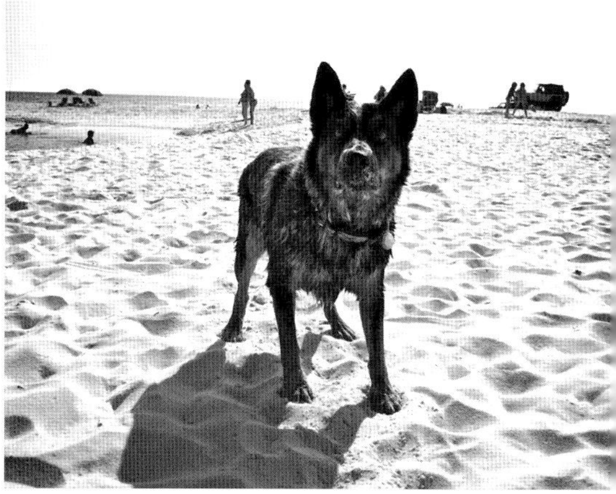

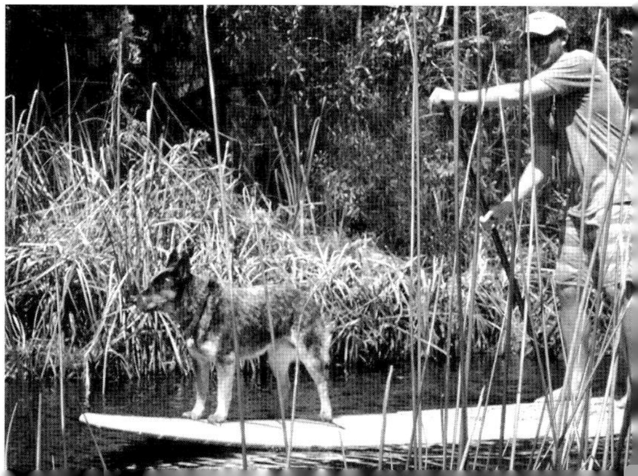

Nip
GRAYTON BEACH
LOVED BY: JUSTIN, STEPHANIE, FOX, & HARLEY NICHOLS

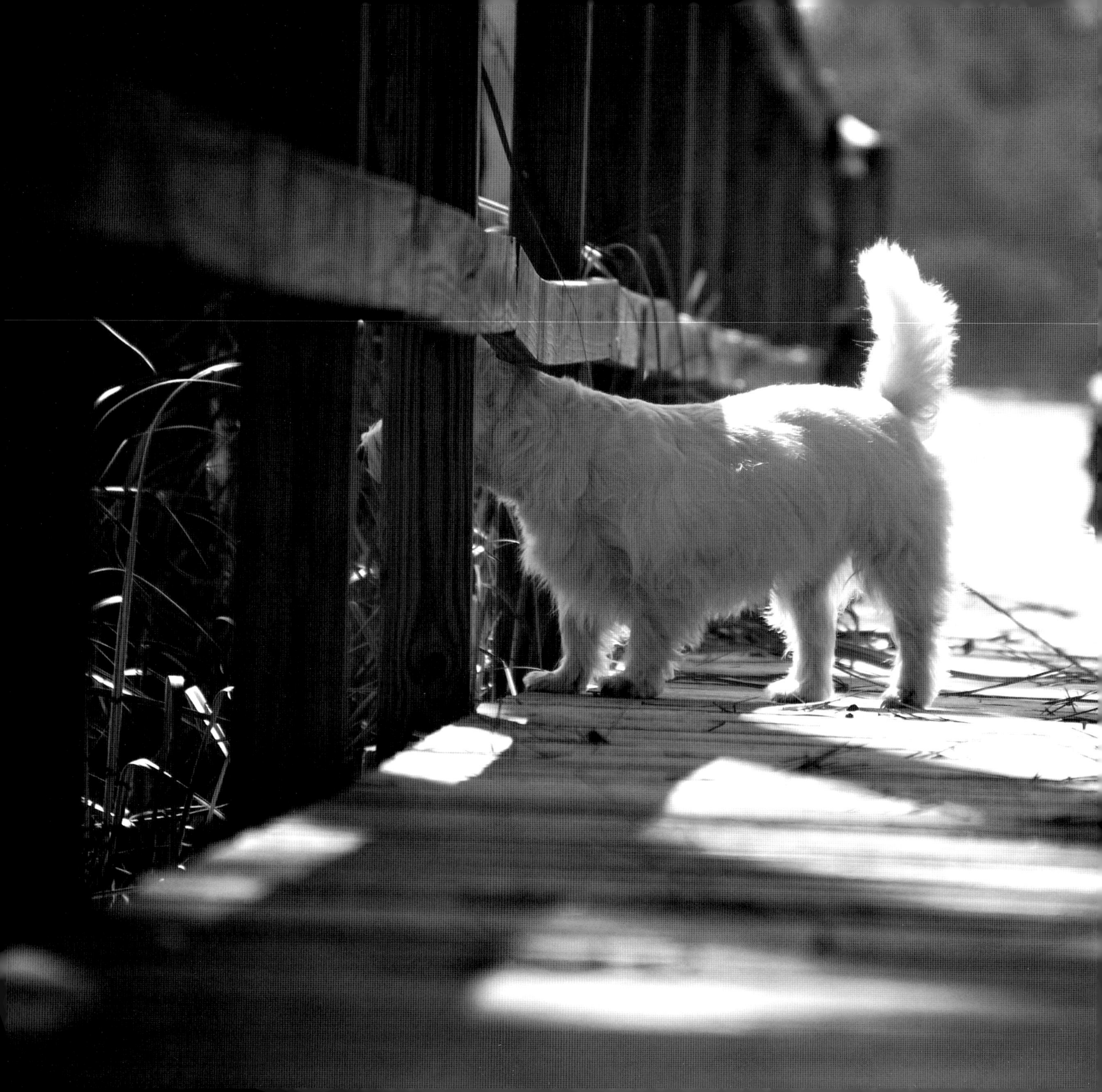

Echo

LaGrange Bayou
Loved by: Barbara Wheeler

"Getting in trouble early in his puppyhood, Echo was bitten by a pygmy rattler not once, but twice, on the same day! Guess he couldn't figure out where the noise was coming from!"

Lucky Dog. 2010 THE DOGS OF 30A

"Coco is our companion extraordinaire and she lights up our world!"

Coco

LaGrange Bayou
Loved by: Jim & Wanda Pitts

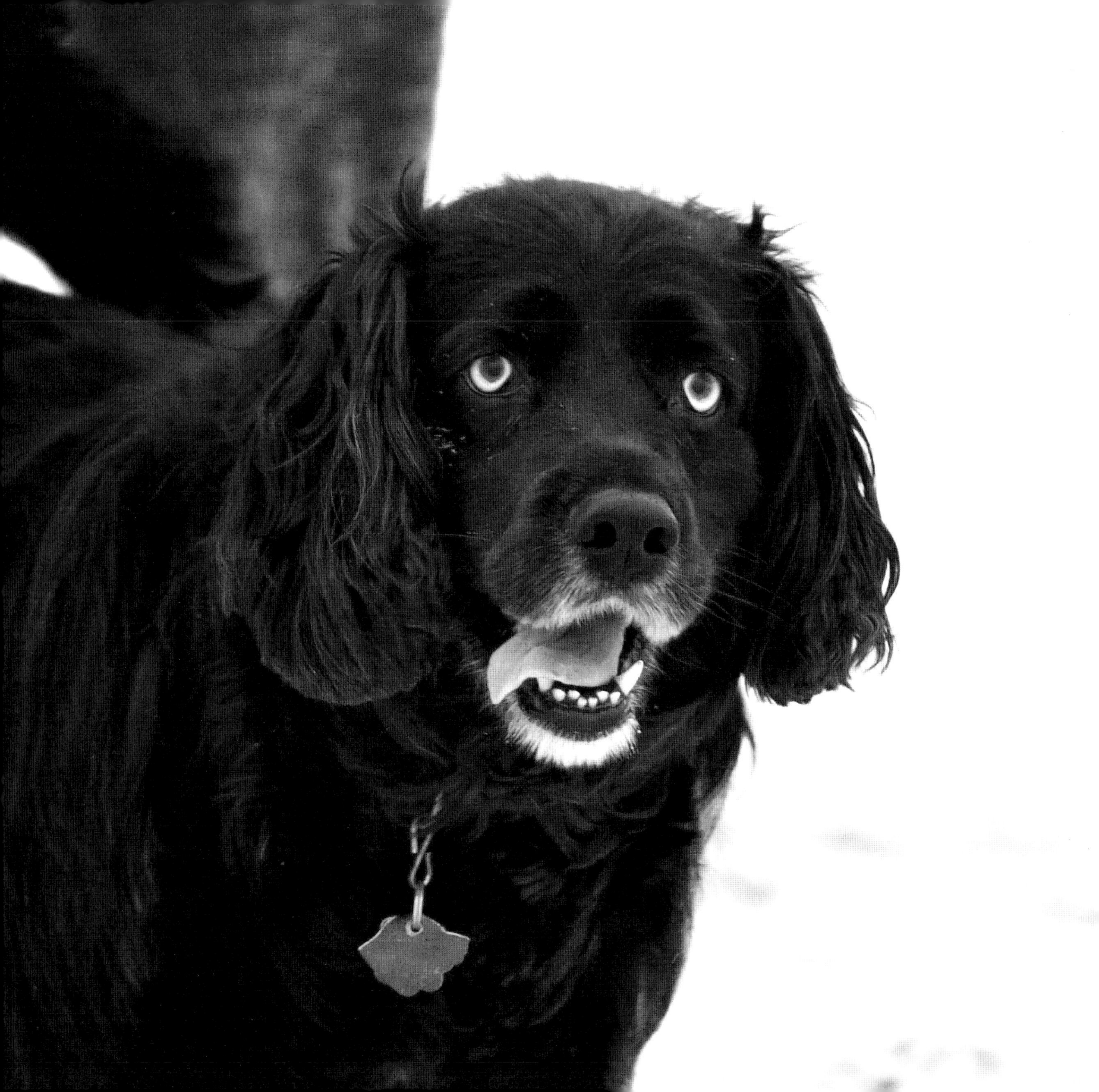

Wendell
Bud & Alley's Pizza Bar
Seaside
Loved by: Rick Daley

Blue
Santa Rosa Beach
Loved by: Keen & Kim Polakoff

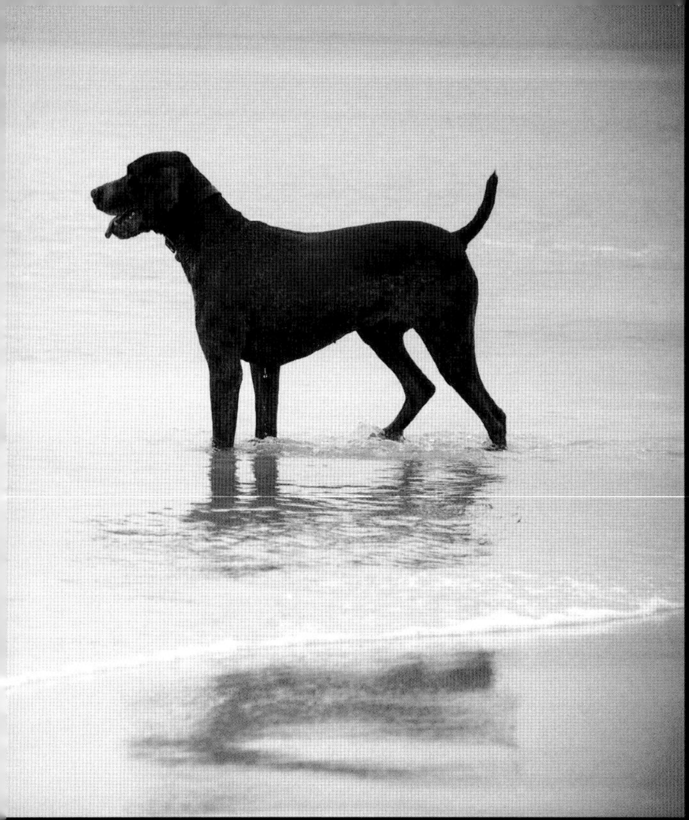
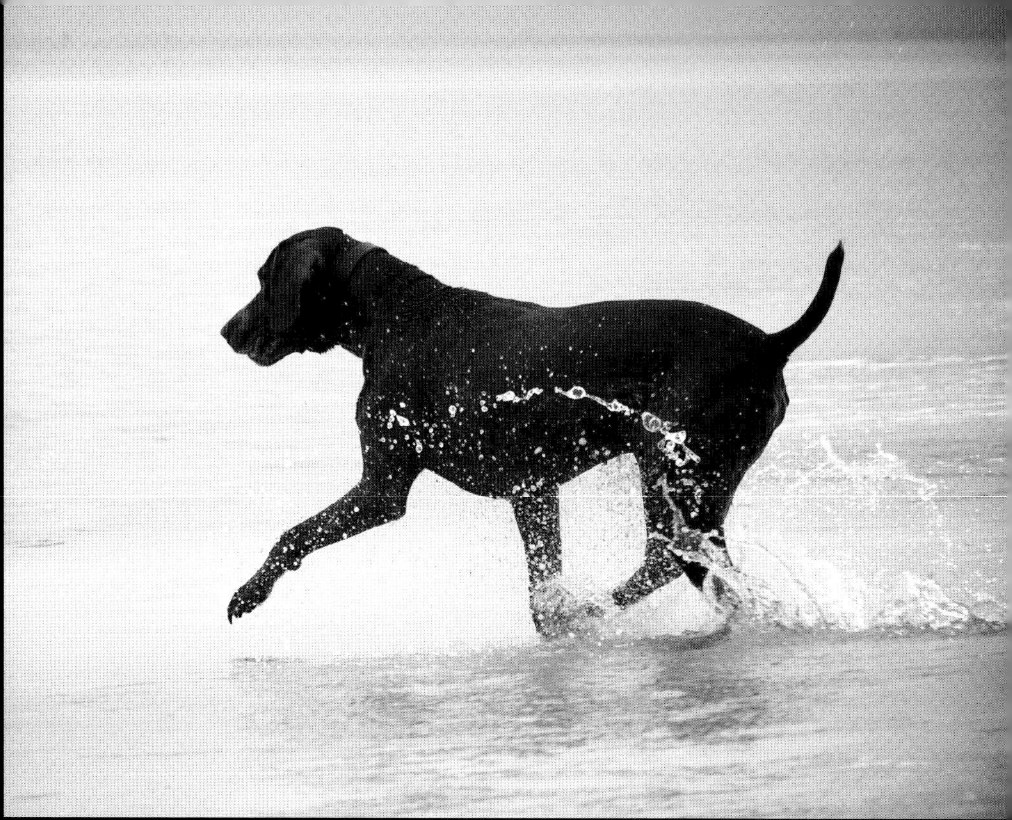
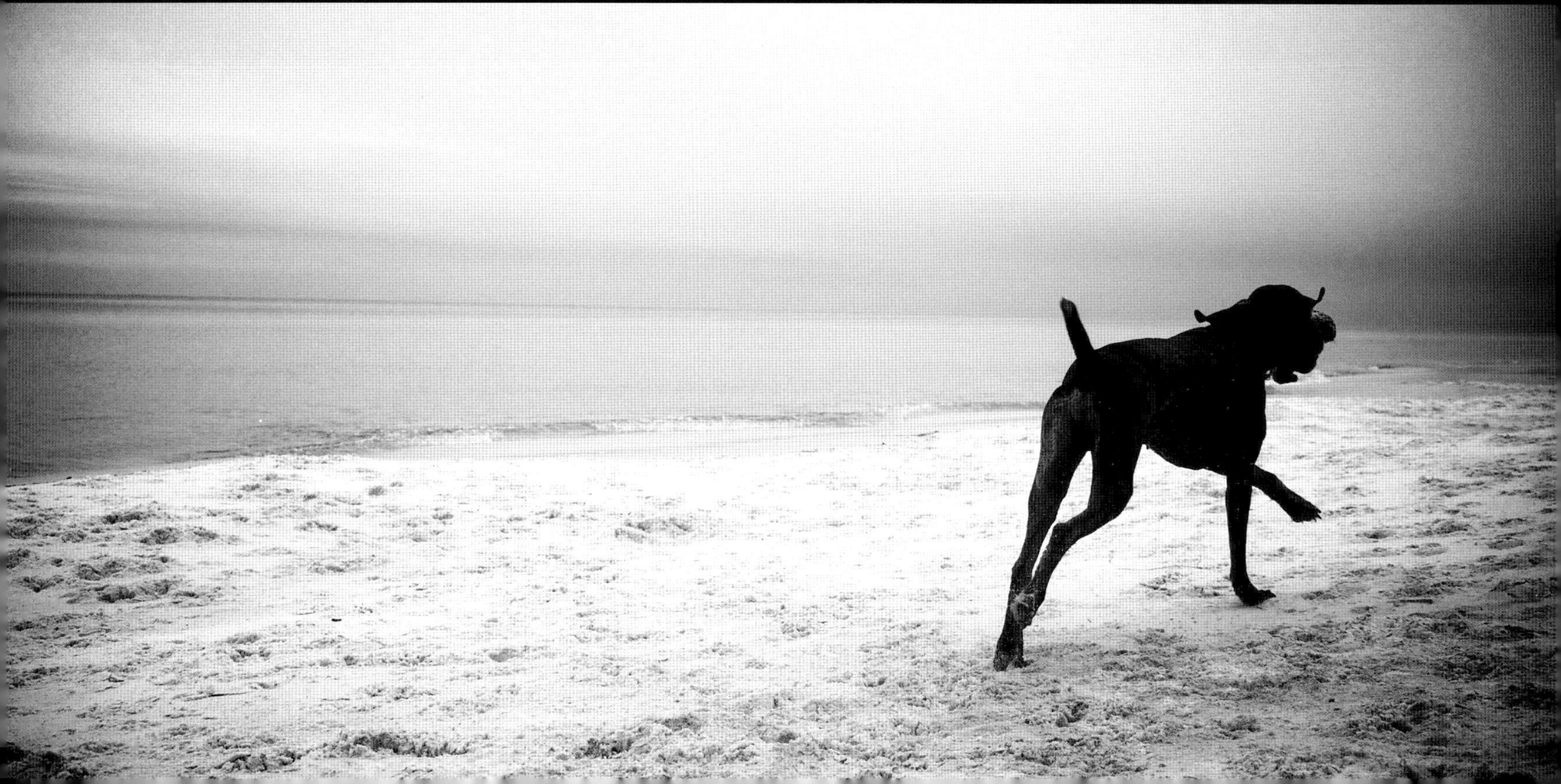

Jack
SANTA ROSA BEACH
LOVED BY: MEG KASPAR

RESCUED
ADOPTED FROM
ALAQUA ANIMAL REFUGE

Suzie

GRAYTON BEACH
LOVED BY: THE O'CALLAGHAN FAMILY

> "He got his name because he is a big 'rock' of muscle."

Boulder

GRAYTON BEACH

LOVED BY: ADAM & REBECCA WILLIAMS

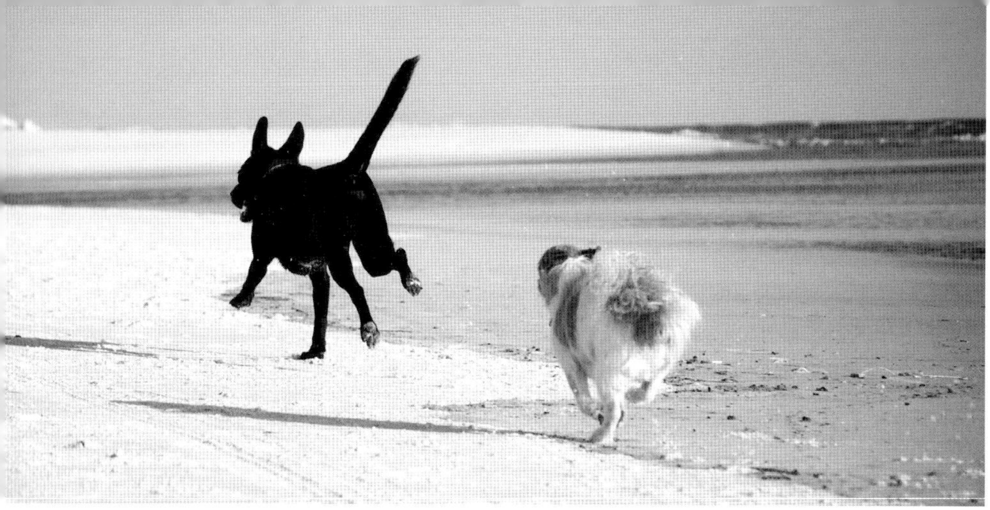

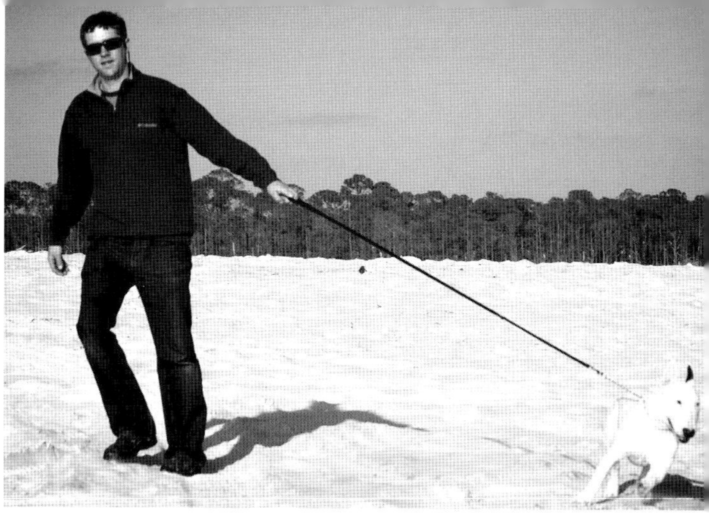

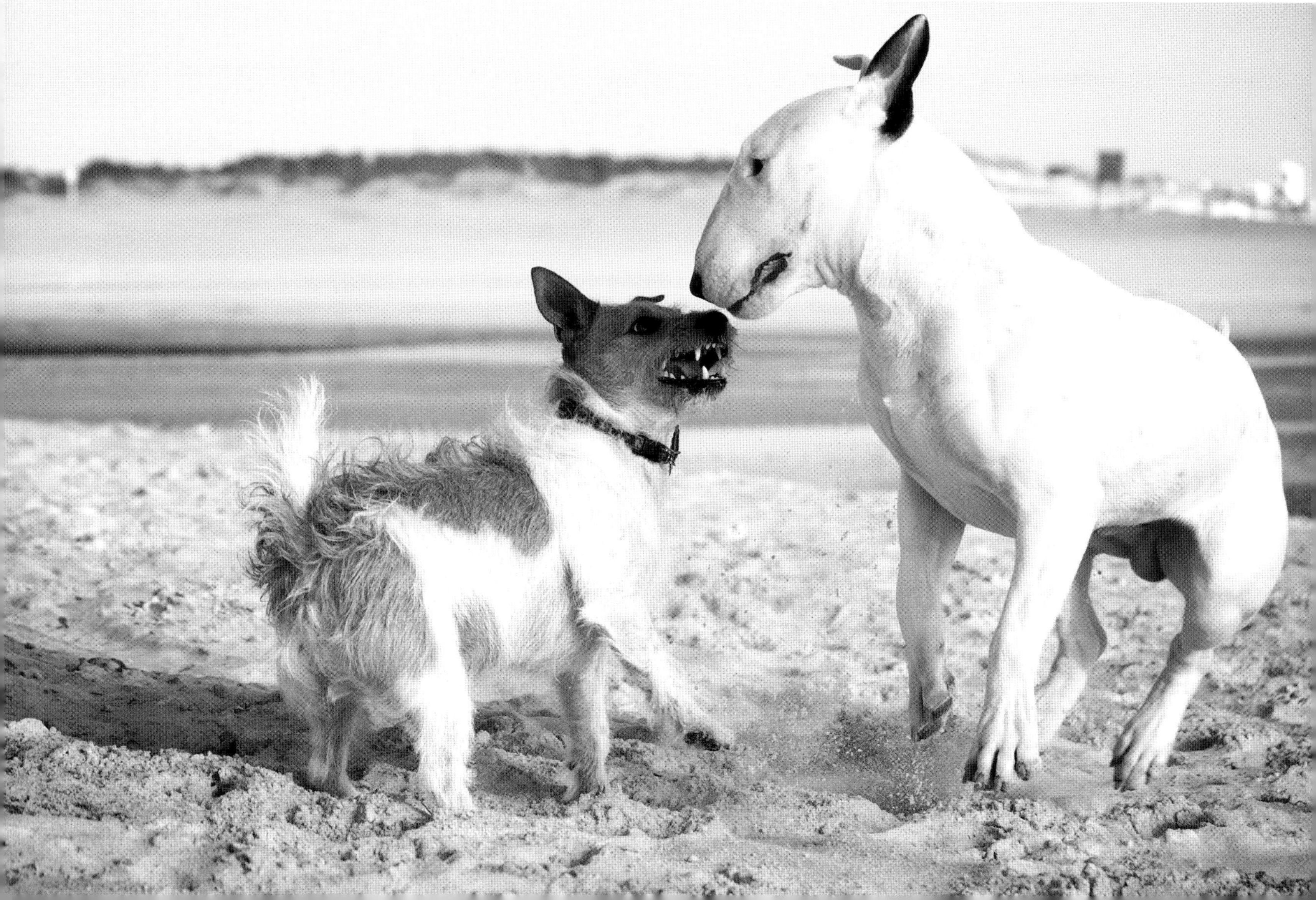

Boulder
GRAYTON BEACH
LOVED BY: ADAM & REBECCA WILLIAMS

Murphee
GRAYTON BEACH
LOVED BY: THE CHAMBERS FAMILY

Augie
GRAYTON BEACH
loved by: CHRISTI FERRY

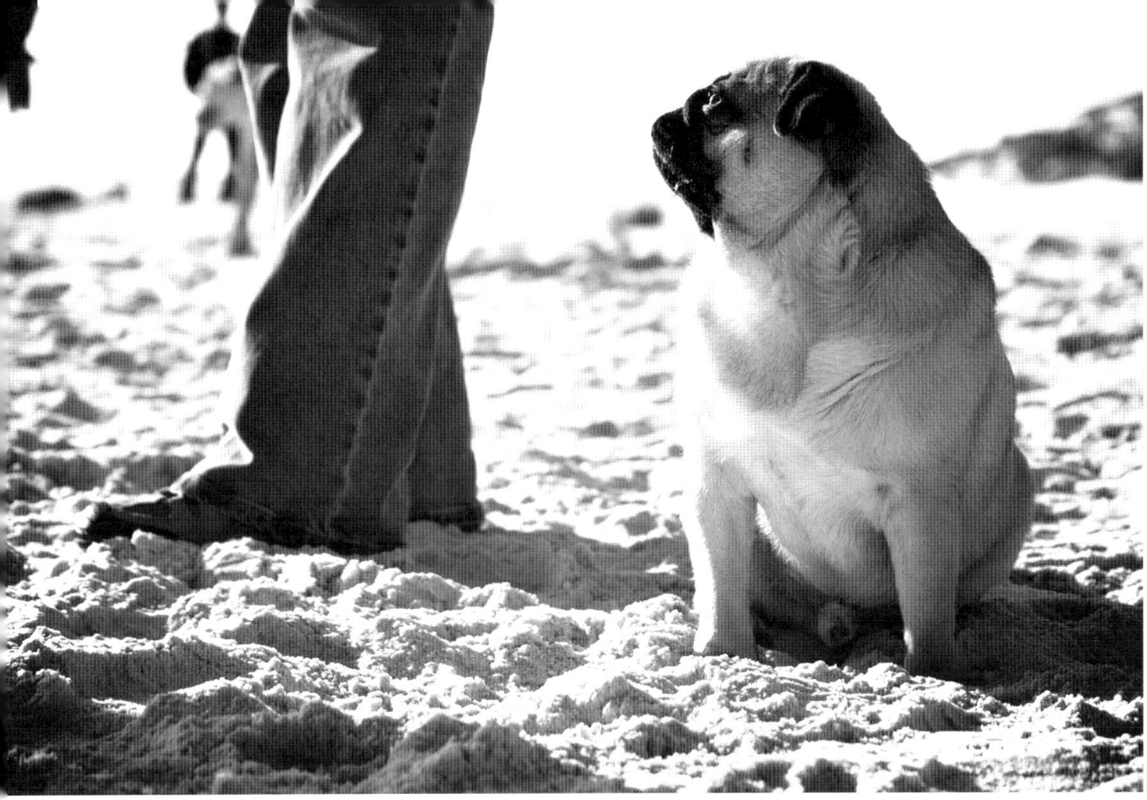
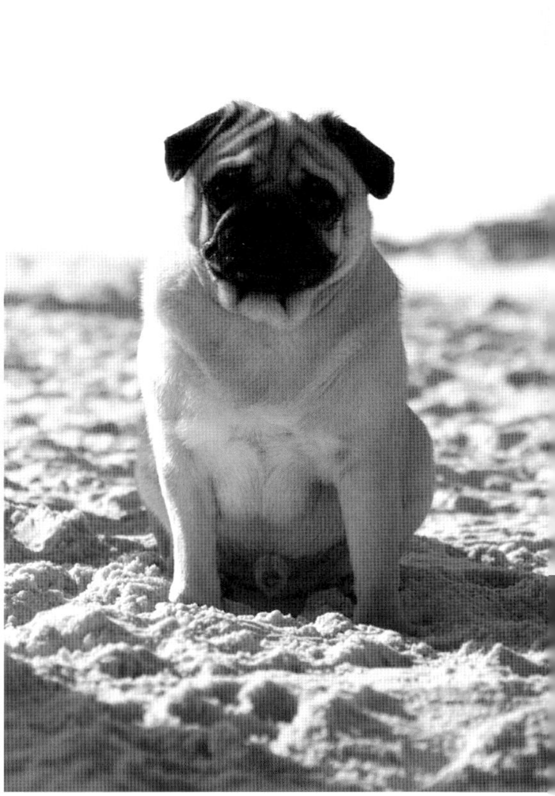
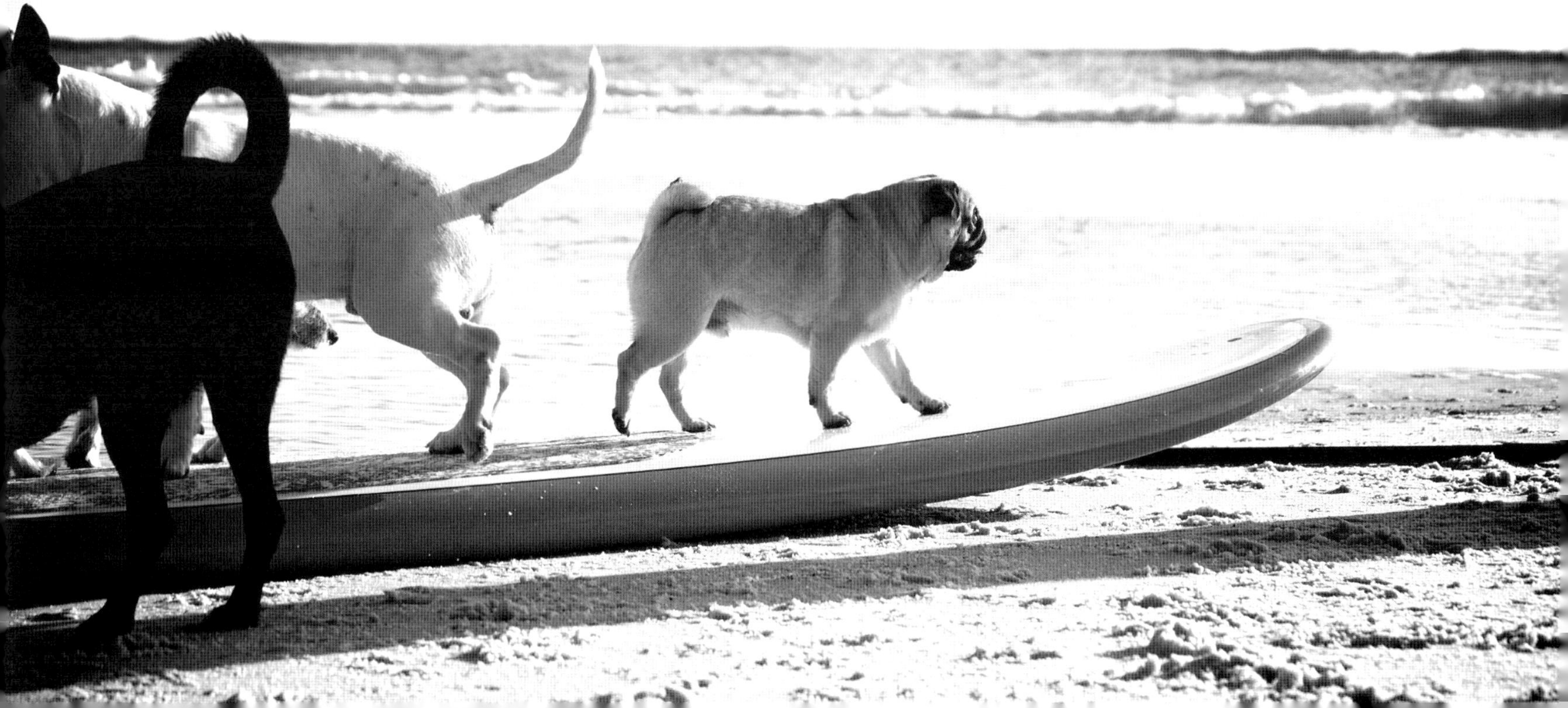

RESCUED
Adopted from
Panhandle Animal Welfare Society
(PAWS), Ft. Walton Beach, Florida

RESCUED
ADOPTED FROM
BARTOW COUNTY HUMANE SOCIETY
CARTERSVILLE, GEORGIA

Leela
SANTA ROSA BEACH
LOVED BY: MARK & MARY ANDREWS

Lizzie
SANTA ROSA BEACH
LOVED BY: MARK & MARY ANDREWS

Lucky Dog. 2010 THE DOGS OF 30A

RESCUED
ADOPTED FROM
THE NASHVILLE ANIMAL SHELTER

"Franny loves chasing squirrels and rabbits (even though they always get away), running with her best bud Pepper and having her Frosty Paws doggie ice cream every night on the couch with us. Around 9:00 every night she gets on 'her square' on the couch and starts asking for this by tapping her tail on the cushion and making a low howling sound until we bring her the ice cream!"

RESCUED
Adopted from CARA, Jackson, Mississippi

Ava
Hotz Avenue Boat Ramp
Grayton Beach
Loved by: Bill, Leigh & Robbie Patterson

> "When Ava gets hungry, she goes into the pantry to see if there is any food on the lower shelves that needs to be 'stored' for later. We have found pilfered hamburger buns under tables, behind chests, and even under our pillows!"

Franny
Sandestin
Loved by: The Durden Family

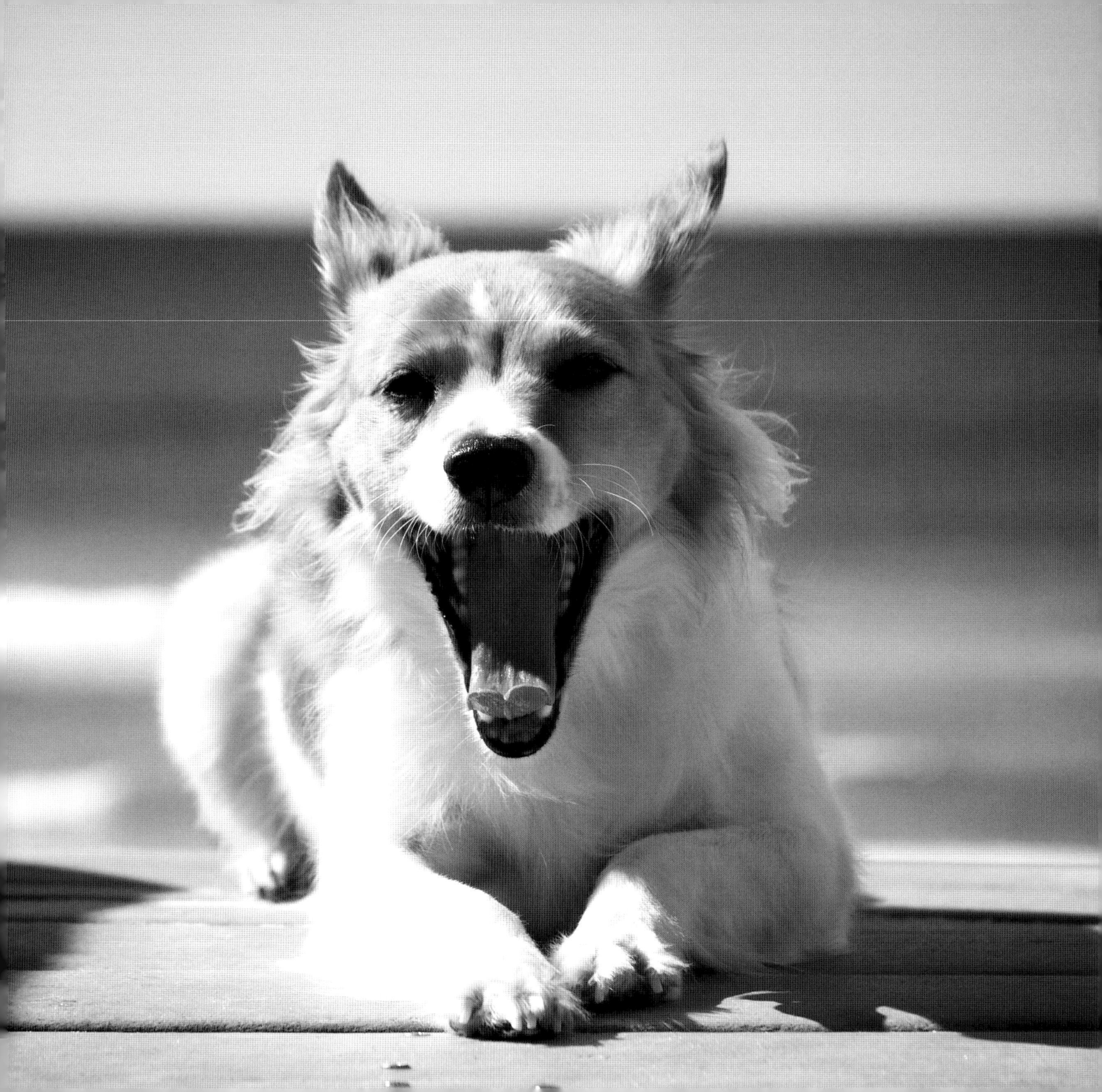

Marley a.k.a. Boo Boo
Santa Rosa Beach
Loved by: Amy & Will Johnson

Lucky Dog. 2010 THE DOGS OF 30A 103

RESCUED
Adopted from
The Siberian Husky Rescue
St. Petersburg, Florida

Bandit & Dallas

Choctawhatchee Bay
Loved by: The O'Donnell Family

RESCUED
ADOPTED FROM
THE SIBERIAN HUSKY RESCUE
ST. PETERSBURG, FLORIDA

Dallas

CHOCTAWHATCHEE BAY
LOVED BY: THE O'DONNELL FAMILY

"Itsy 'owns' the Red Bird Gallery. She sits on a pillow on a bench in front of the gallery and waits for people to walk by. She expects to be petted, and if someone walks by without taking a moment to reach over the fence and tell her how wonderful she is, she will bark at them until they rectify the situation! When Itsy gets tired of lounging in the sun, she works her way back into the gallery and asks me to put her in the desk drawer (second from the top), which is lined with a fluffy dog bed. She's a working dog, however, and has to pull her weight. Itsy's job is to entertain the children while their parents peruse the gallery, and she is always right on task!"

"I call her Yahweh's little love-gift to me."

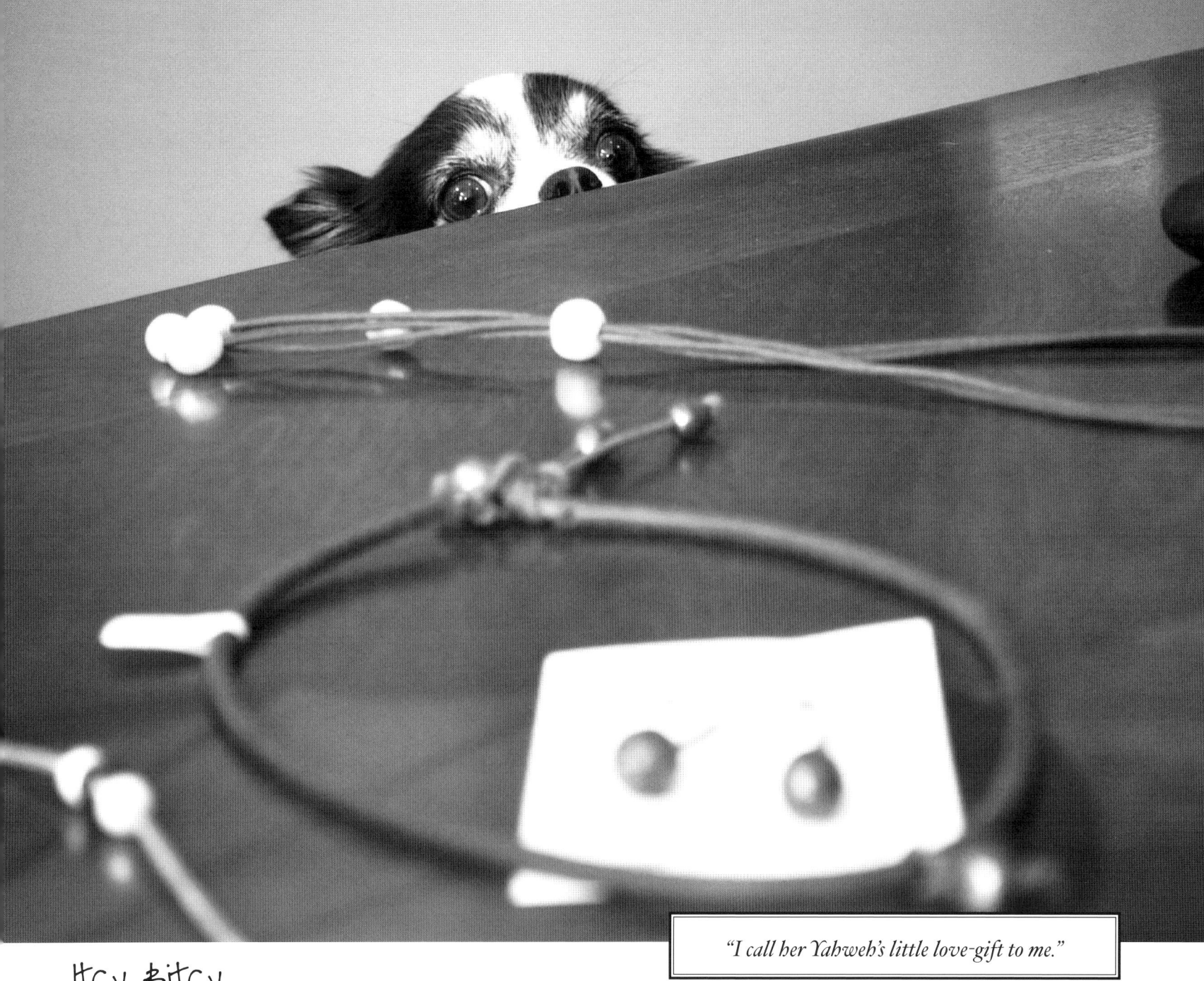

Itsy Bitsy

RED BIRD GALLERY
SEASIDE'S RUSKIN PLACE ARTIST COLONY
SEASIDE
LOVED BY: TRICIA MOORE

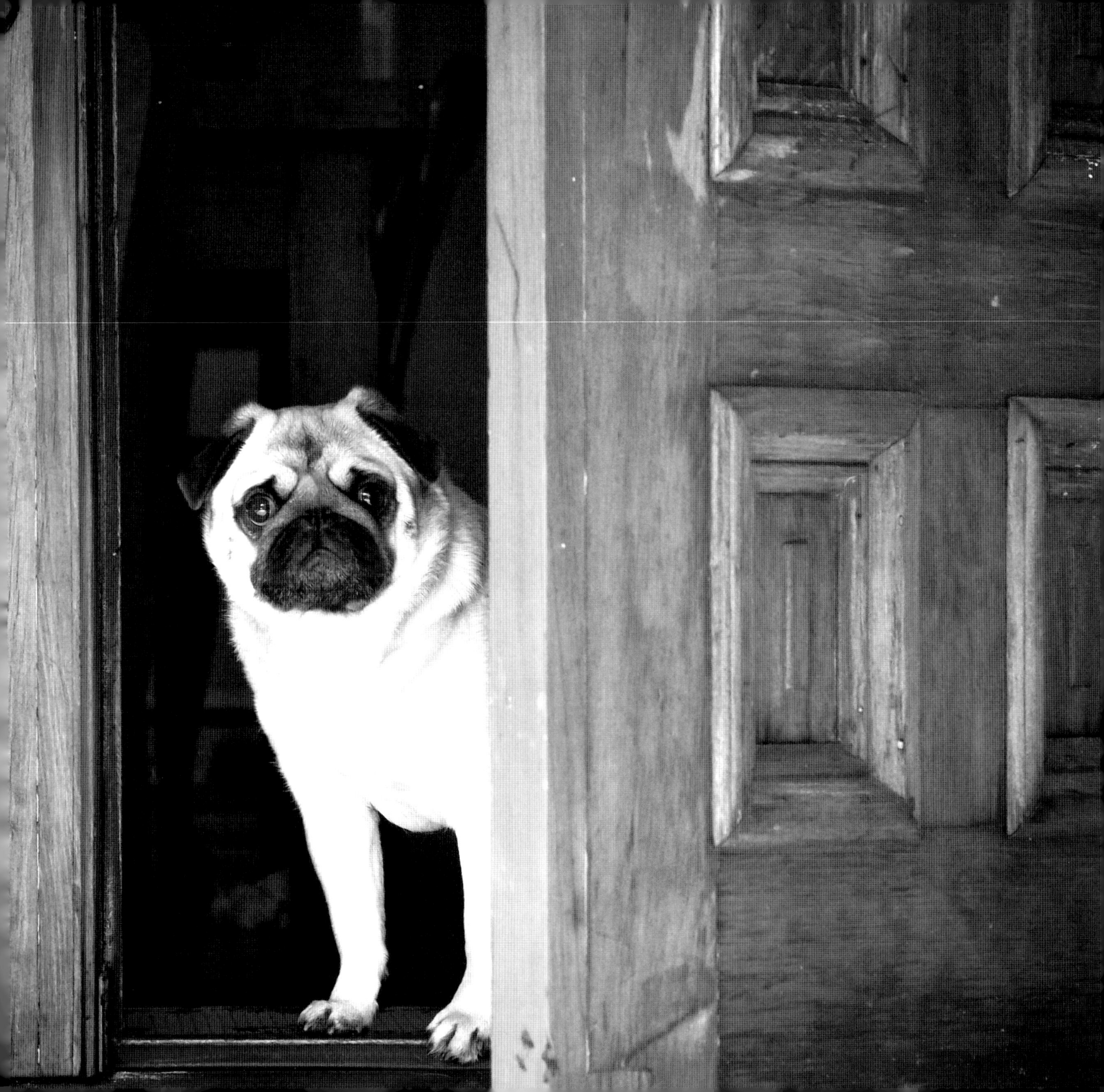

Oliver
Old Seagrove
Loved by: Dr. Phil & Susan Benton & Reed & Caroline

Peppi
SEASIDE
LOVED BY: THE ARTIGUES FAMILY

RESCUED
From Interstate
I-10, Florida

King Tut
"THE DEFENSE RESTS"
BLUE MOUNTAIN BEACH
LOVED BY: THE GEORGE RALPH MILLER FAMILY

> "We had caught glimpses of King Tut in the middle of I-10 for two days in a row, cowering in the rain without shelter, and intently watching each passing car. On the third day, the weather broke, and we decided to try to coax him into our car. Terrified, he finally crawled into our car, shivering and crouching behind our children in the back seat. He had survived bitter cold and thunderstorms and no food, water, or shelter, was emaciated, and had several broken ribs. His luck changed when he took a chance and got in that car."

Mike

"The defense rests"
Blue Mountain Beach
Loved by: The George Ralph Miller Family

Isabelle
"THE DEFENSE RESTS"
BLUE MOUNTAIN BEACH
LOVED BY: THE GEORGE RALPH MILLER FAMILY

"When I met Daisy for the first time she had just gotten back from being spayed at the vet, was shaved and sad-looking, and very forlorn after her twenty-nine day stay at PAWS.

I knew right away that she was 'my' dog, but I think it took her a couple days to realize that her nightmare was over, and that I was 'her' person... forever."

Daisy

SEASIDE REPERTORY THEATRE (THE REP)
SEASIDE
LOVED BY: CAROL GAGLIARDI

RESCUED
Adopted from
Underdogs of Destin

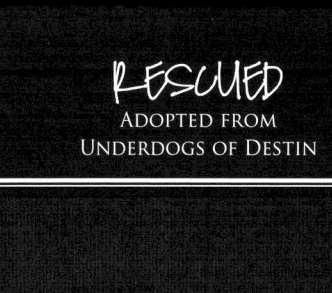

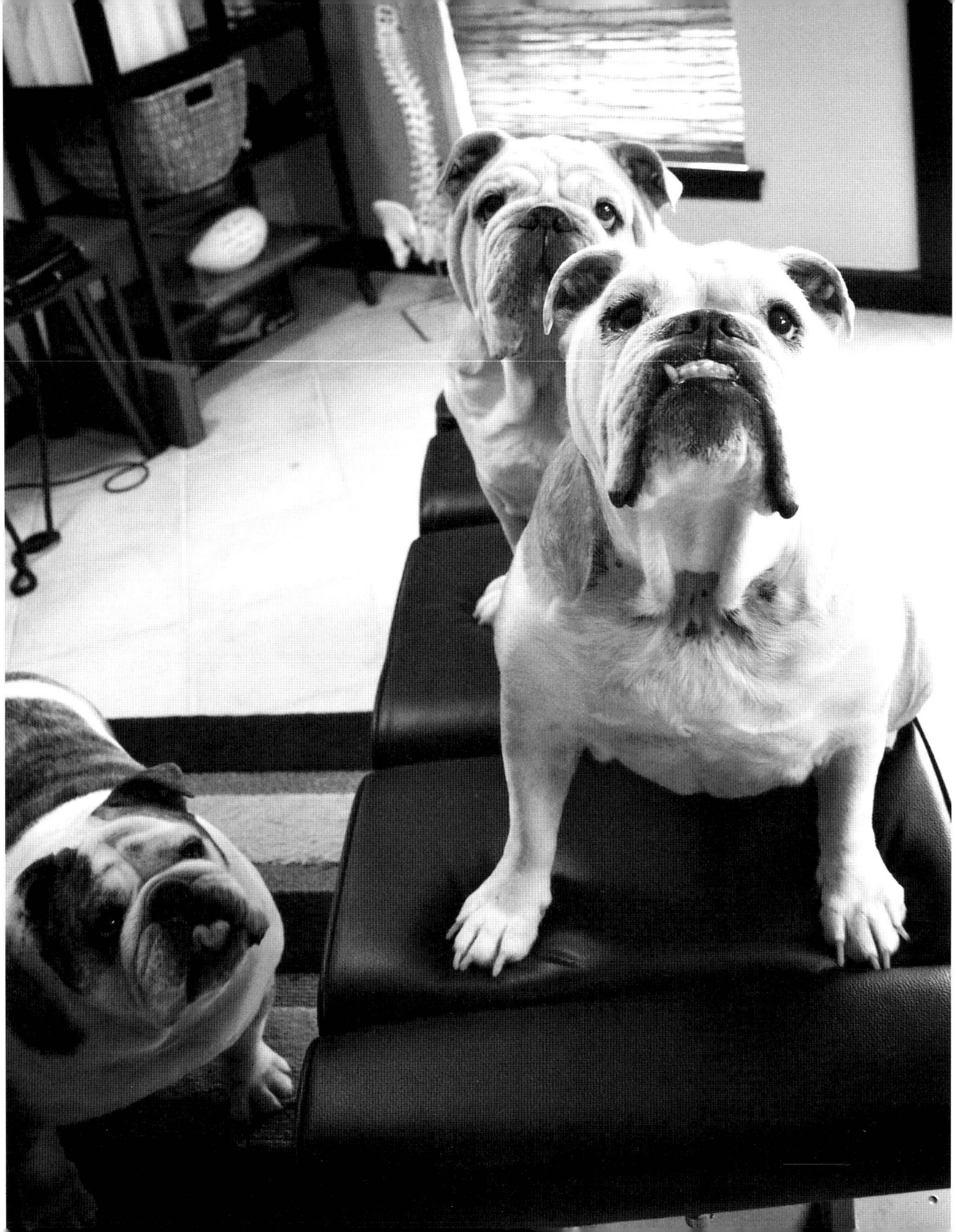

Norman, Mr. Biggs & Cooper
Balance Health Studio
Seagrove Beach
Loved by: Bart & Kelli Precourt

Lucky Dog. 2010 THE DOGS OF 30A

Larry

BALANCE HEALTH STUDIO
SEAGROVE BEACH
LOVED BY: GILLIAN & GERRY LEE

Mojo

Arriaga Originals
Seacrest
Loved by: Shellie & Richard Arriaga

Ziggy & Buddy
Rosemary Beach
Loved by: Robin, Russell & Sarah Beans

The Dogs of 30A Lucky Dog. 2010

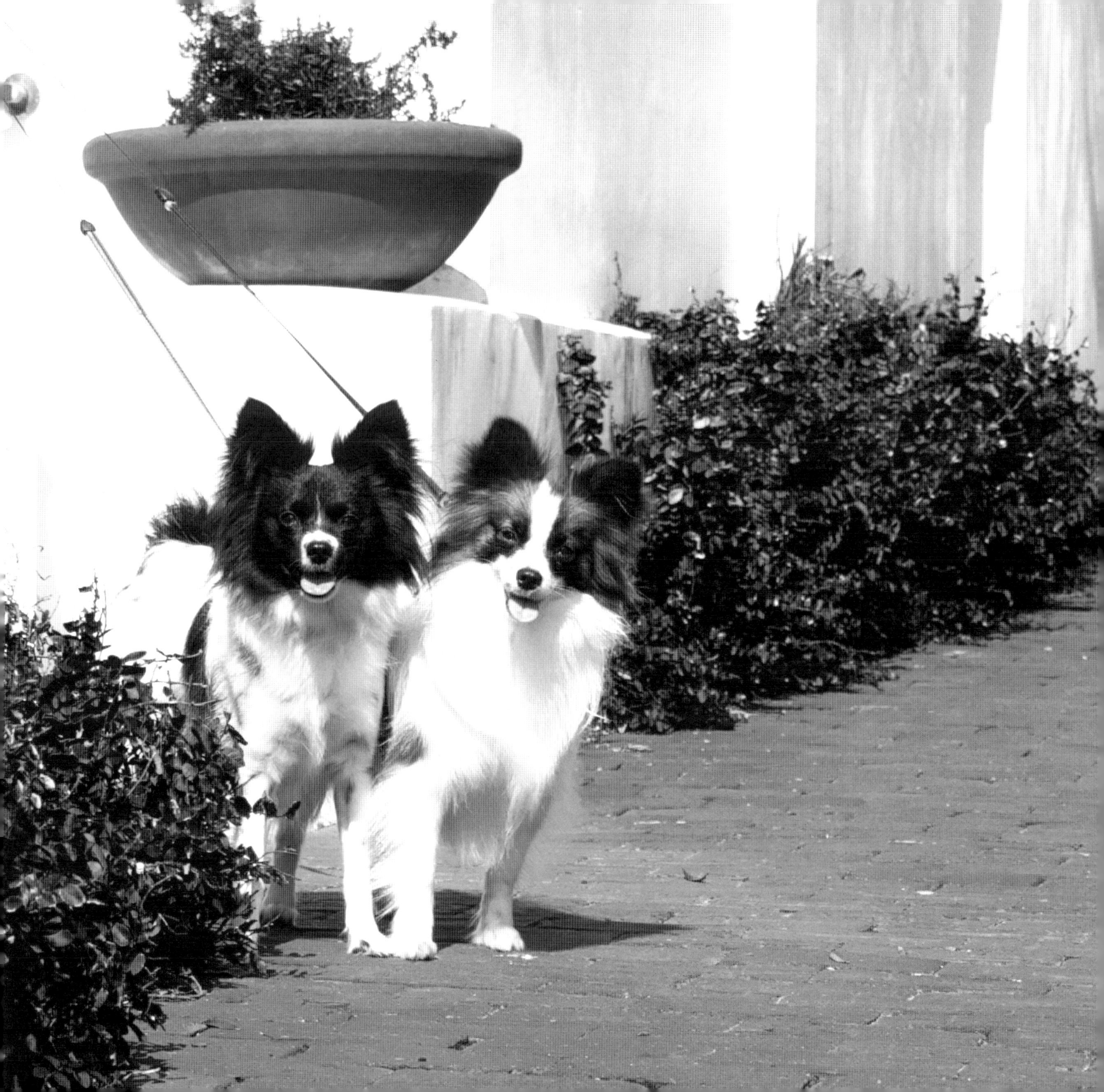

Brucie

Rosemary Beach
Loved by: Tom & Mary Butler

Buppie

Rosemary Beach
Loved by: Tom & Mary Butler

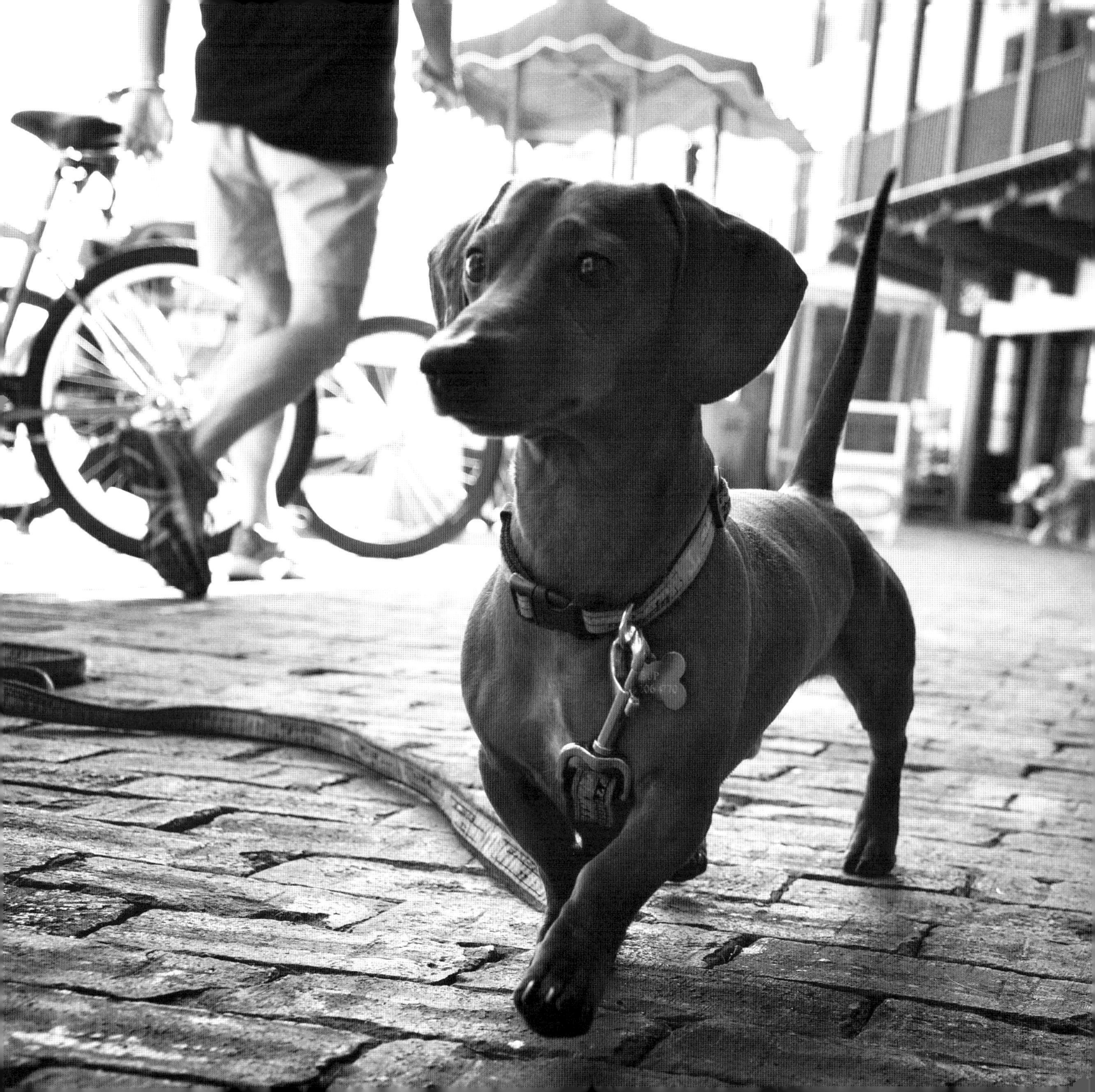

Syrah
SEASIDE

LOVED BY: TERESA ARTIGUES VUCOVICH

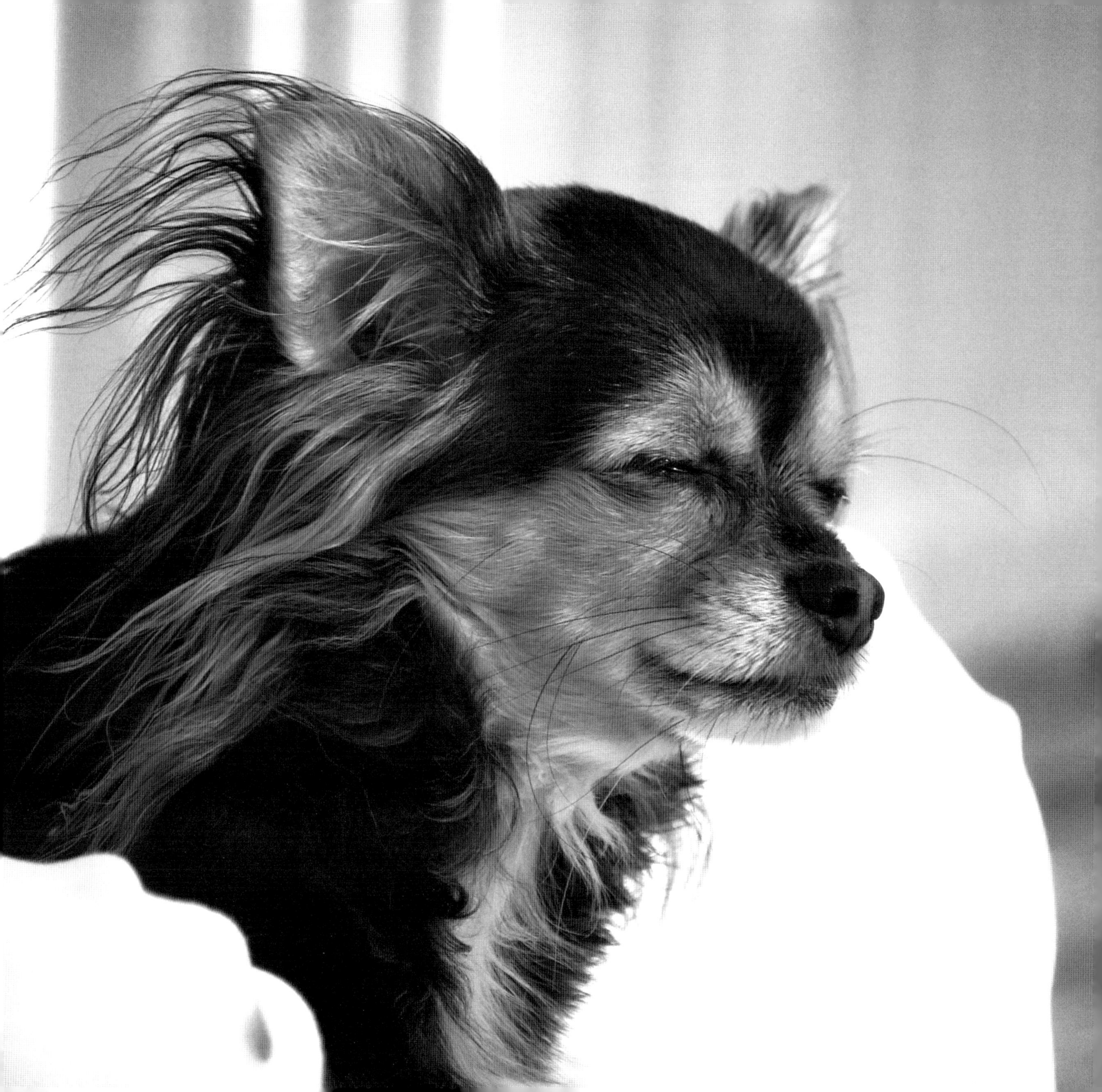

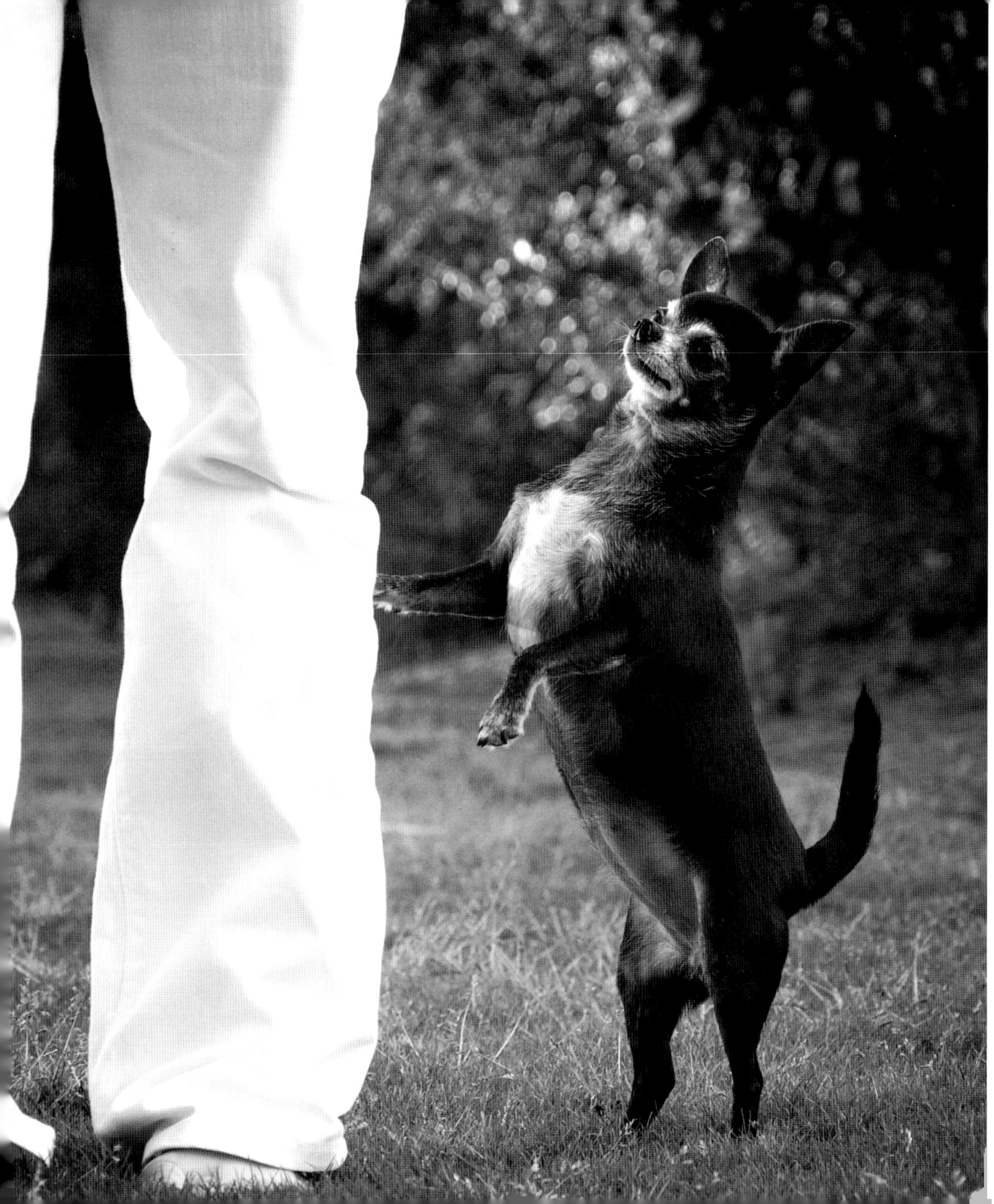

Pinot

SEASIDE
LOVED BY: TERESA ARTIGUES VUCOVICH

Lambert
WATERBUGS
WATERCOLOR
LOVED BY: TAMMY & JAN PERKINS

Lambert & Bettis

The Watercolor Store
Watercolor
Loved by: Tammy & Jan Perkins

Sadie
a.k.a.
Slim Shaky

WaterBugs
Watercolor
Loved by: Nancy McCullen

Milly
SEAGROVE BEACH
LOVED BY: BARBARA & LEE ROWAN

"Milly has big shoes to fill, and with those feet, it's an easy task!"

> "I met the lady the next day expecting to pick up my Doberman-look-alike and was extremely surprised to see a 'little old man' looking out of the window!"

Schwood

THE RETREAT
BLUE MOUNTAIN BEACH
LOVED BY: ALEC & AMBER BREAUD

Pirogue
THE RETREAT
BLUE MOUNTAIN BEACH
LOVED BY: ALEC & AMBER BREAUD

"Pirogue learned slowly and grew quickly."

Lucky Dog. 2010   THE DOGS OF 30A

Paris

Cerulean Park
Watercolor
Loved by: Mary Janice Lemaire

Pilar

CERULEAN PARK
WATERCOLOR
LOVED BY: TIFFANY CURRID

King
PATCHOULI'S
ROSEMARY BEACH
LOVED BY: LYNN DUGAS

> "King has been given a few nicknames, 'Licky Noodles' being one when the boys were younger, because he licks constantly: the air, a leg, his pillow, you name it!"

"Blondie always says hello with a nudge, in 'the front' and in 'the back.' She can't help that her height is just right there!"

RESCUED
ADOPTED FROM
PET ANIMAL WELFARE SOCIETY
(PAWS)

Blondie
PATCHOULI'S
ROSEMARY BEACH
LOVED BY: LYNN DUGAS

Georgia Bear
Gulf Place Town Center
Santa Rosa Beach
Loved by: Helen Irving

Lucky Dog. 2010

> RESCUED
> SAVED FROM
> AN ABUSIVE HOME

Kazie

SANTA ROSA BEACH

LOVED BY: KELLY & ROBERT CORNELIUS

Louie

La Crema
Rosemary Beach
Loved by: Kevin, Kim, Hannah, Sam, & Anderson Neel

Teensie

Amoré by the Sea
Seaside's Ruskin Place Artist Colony
Seaside
Loved by: Rino & Melanie Scicluna & Kellon Campbell

Kahlua Roux
ROSEMARY BEACH
LOVED BY: CAROL & KEVIN MCDUGLE

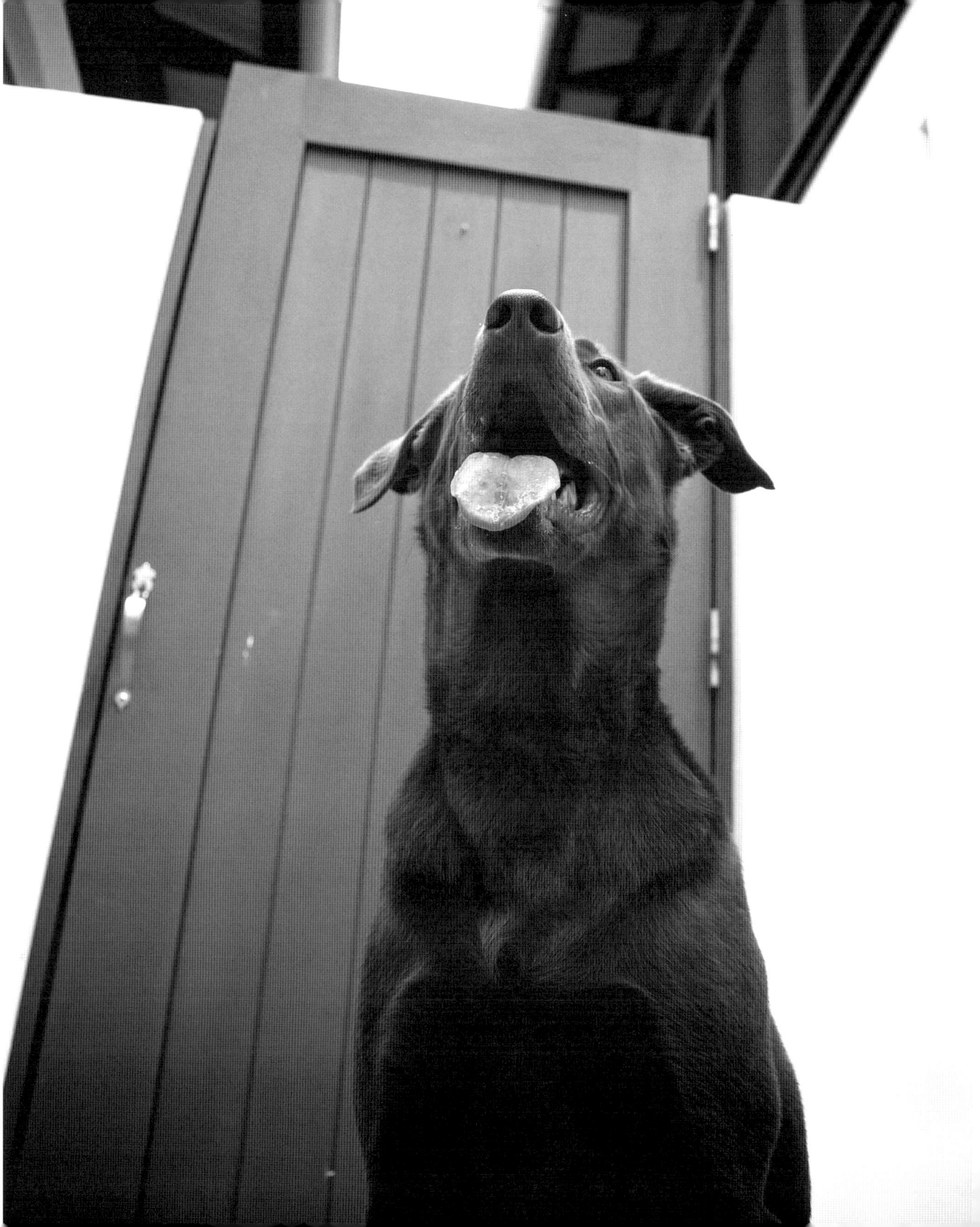

Gumbo
SOUTHWINDS III
SANDESTIN
LOVED BY: SHANE & RICK HILL & "HER GIRL" JORDAN

Lucky Dog. 2010

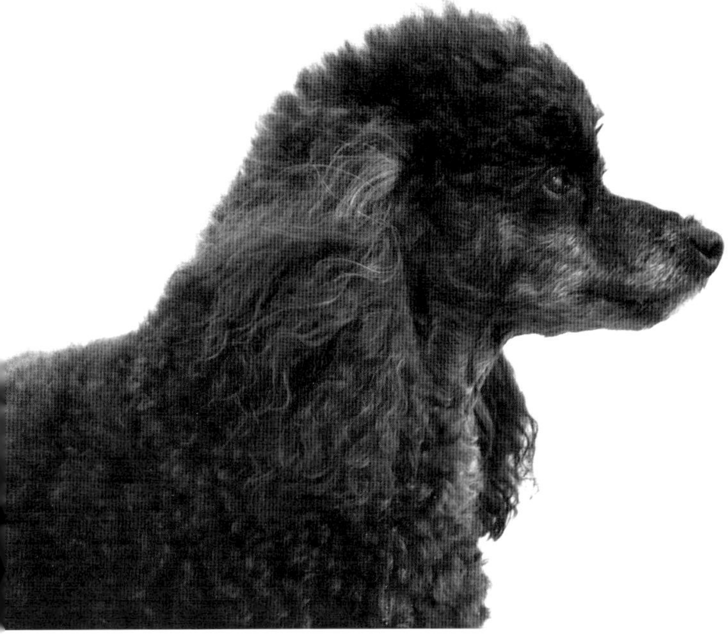
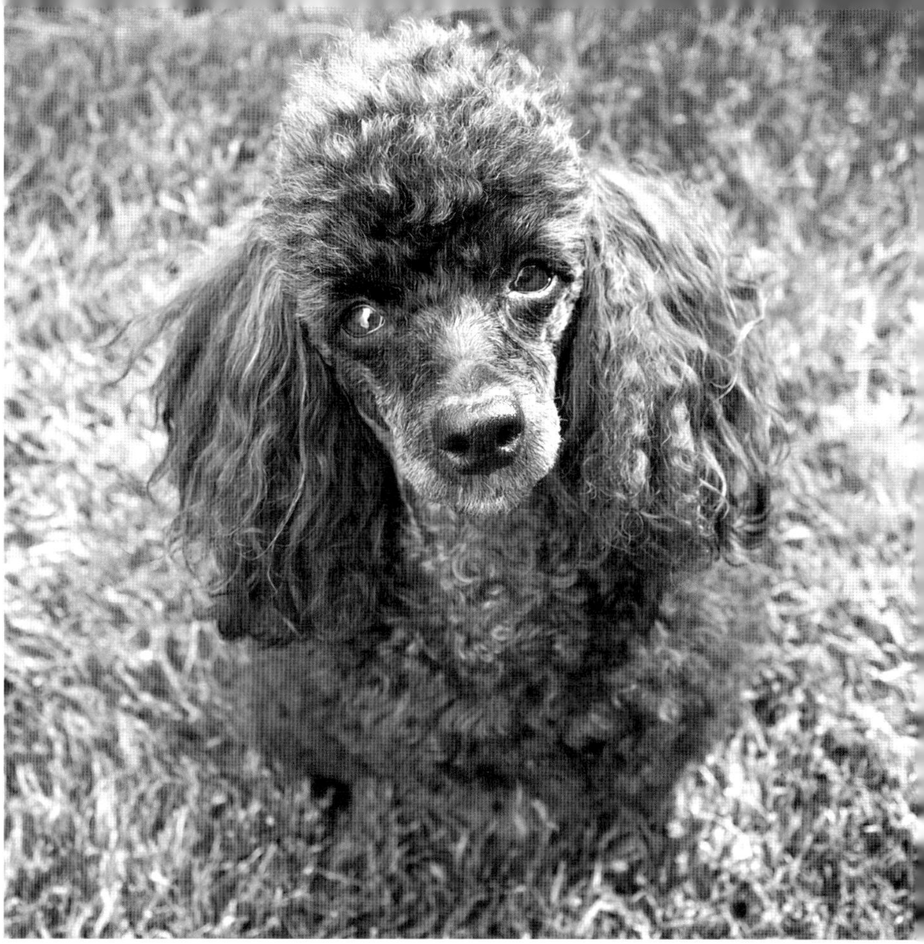
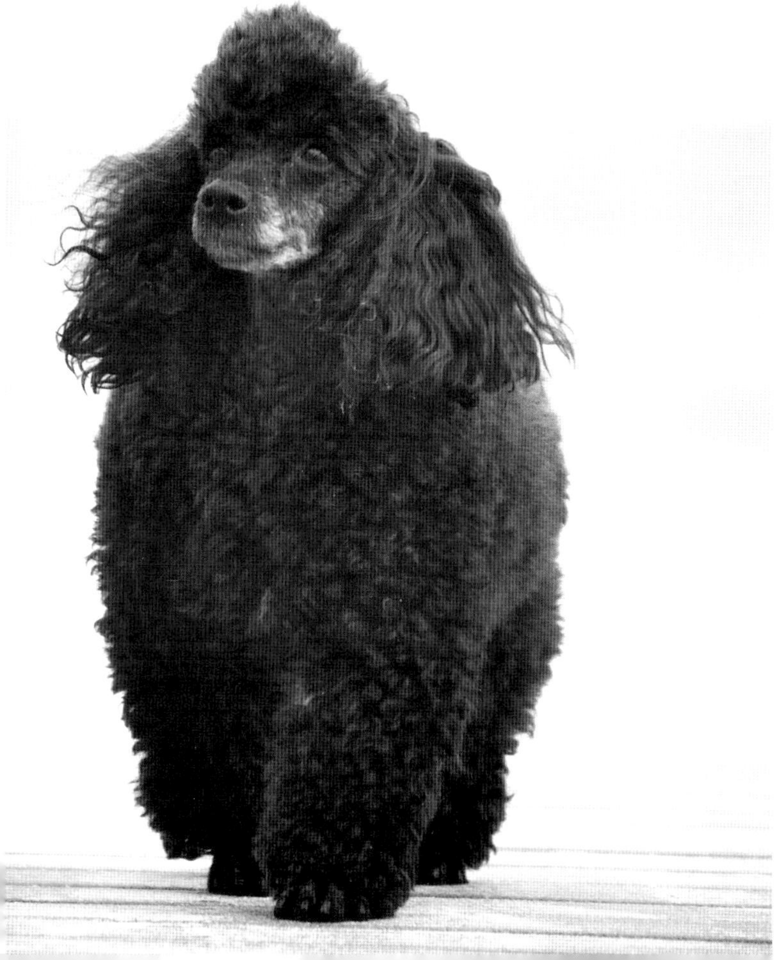
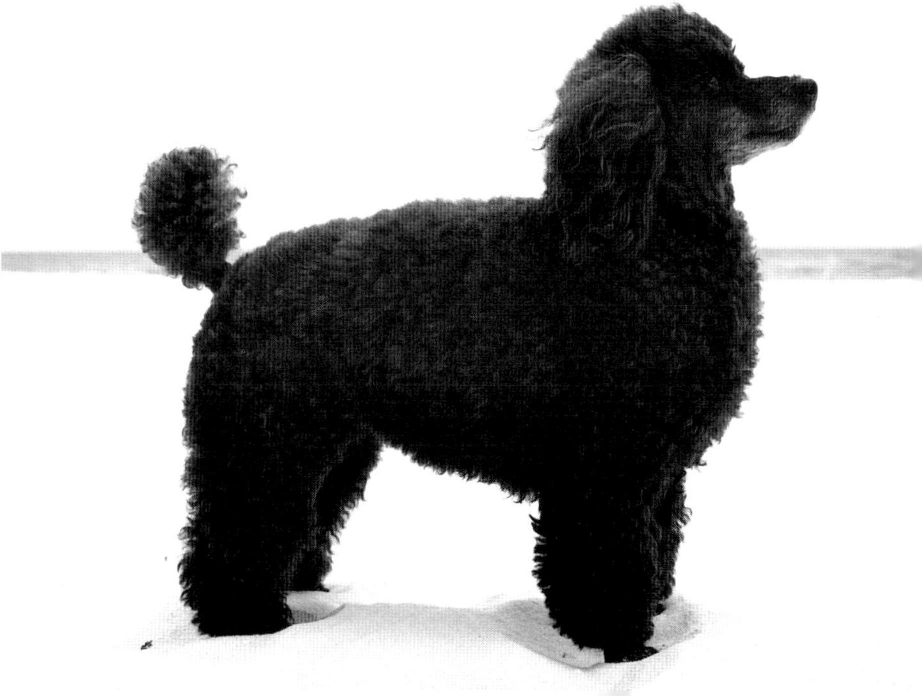

Casey

Grayton Beach
Loved by: The Craft Family

Max

Grayton Beach
Loved by: The Craft Family

Rescued
Adopted from
Alaqua animal Refuge

Hula

Grayton Beach

Loved by: Donnie, Jennifer, Makensie, Allyson & Kaya Sundal

RESCUED
FROM
THE BARK PARK

"Early Bird is a true mutt who was found at The Bark Park with his five brothers. We were able to adopt them all out the weekend of the Super Bowl at Shorty's in Grayton Beach. The locally famous 'Who Dat' Dogs!"

Early Bird
GRAYTON BEACH
LOVED BY: DONNIE, JENNIFER, MAKENSIE, ALLYSON & KAYA SUNDAL

"All we knew about Chihuahua's was that they were a pain in the rear: little 'yappers!' Our son took an online test for 'dog matching' and his score revealed that our family's lifestyle was a perfect match for a Chihuahua. Go figure. After laughing hysterically, then retaking the test three times, we reconsidered. Long story short, we brought home our sweet boy, Rocky, almost eight years ago, and where we go, he goes... yapper and all!"

Rocky

SEAGROVE BEACH

LOVED BY: JIM, TARA, BO HARTLEY, JOHN MAJOR & CHRISTIAN DAVIS

Mac

Great Southern Cafe
Seaside
Loved by: Mary Jane Parrish

Luke

Karian Residence
Sandestin
Loved by: The Karian Family

Buddy & Luke

Karian Residence
Sandestin
Loved by: The Karian Family

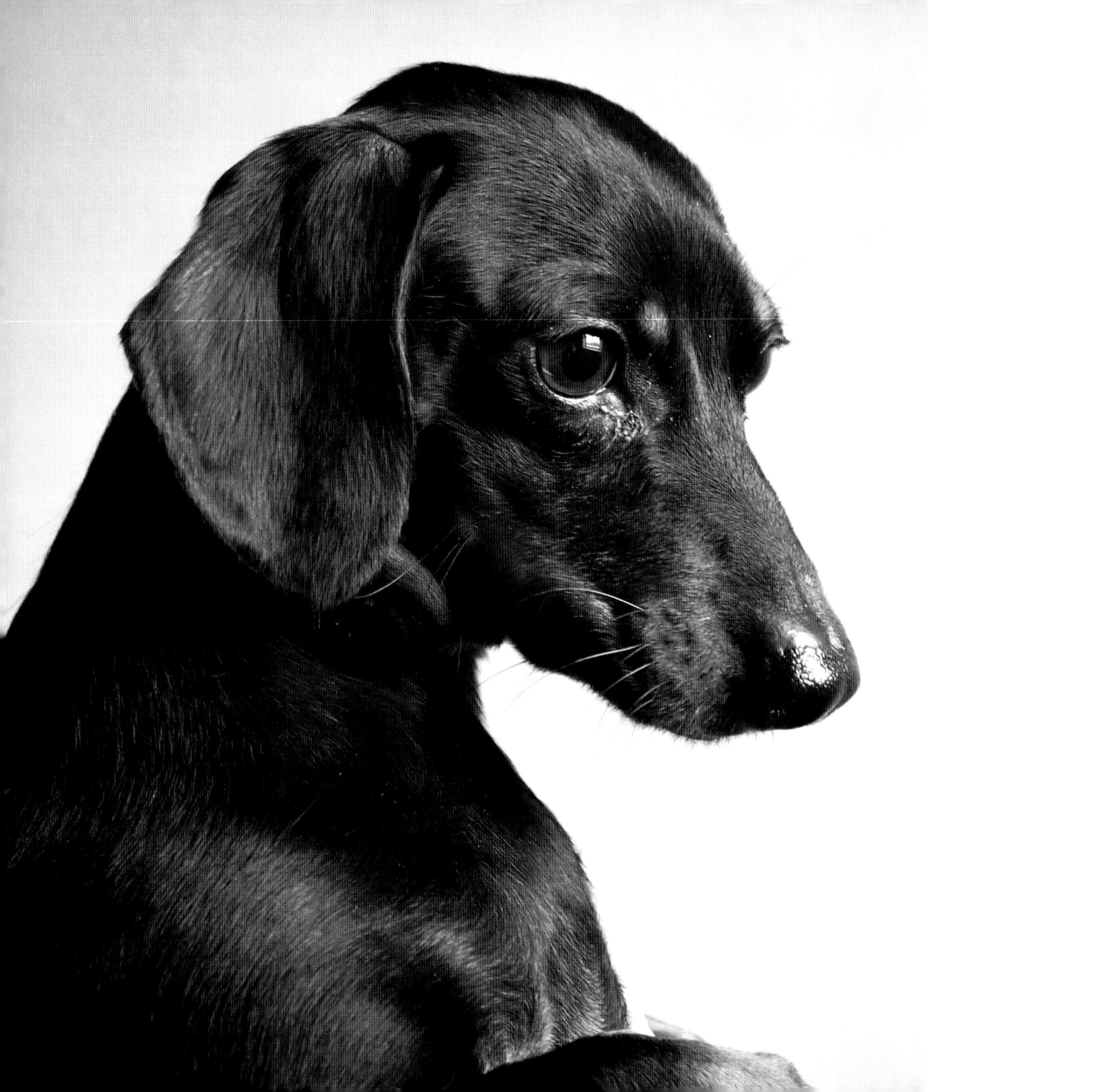

Penny

SANTA ROSA BEACH

LOVED BY: LINDSAY HEDGLIN & CHRISTOPHER, KIM & STEFANI PALL

Lucky Dog. 2010   THE DOGS OF 30A   155

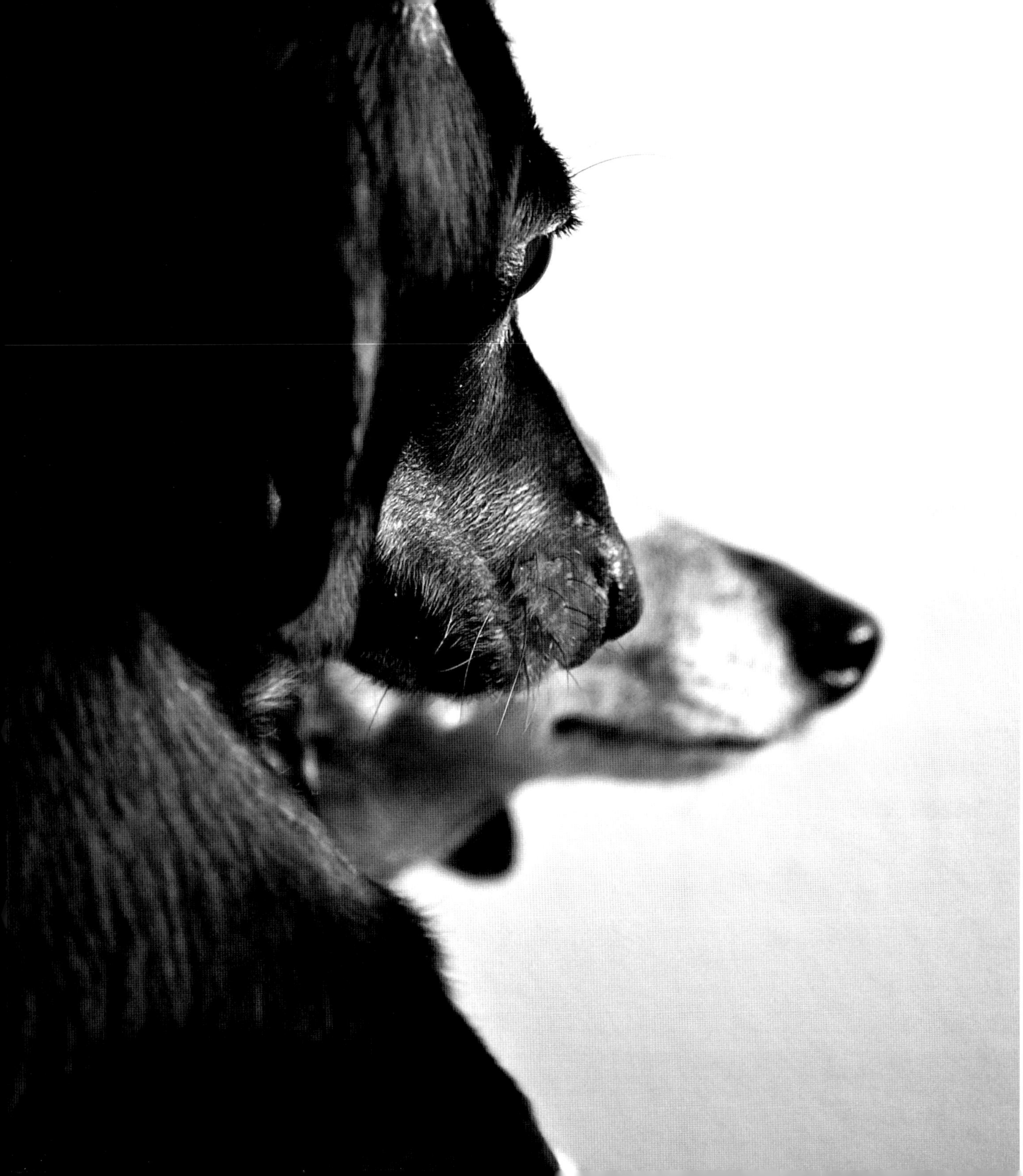

Dixie

Santa Rosa Beach
Loved by: Christopher, Kim & Stefani Pall

Sophia & Livy

CHILDREN'S VOLUNTEER HEALTH NETWORK
SANTA ROSA BEACH
LOVED BY: TRICIA NORTHCUTT

Darby

GULF PLACE TOWN CENTER
SANTA ROSA BEACH
LOVED BY: LORI BRUNSON-SMITH

Zeus

SOUTH WALTON HIGH SCHOOL
LOVED BY: ALICE STAPLETON & KEVIN CIPRIANI

160   THE DOGS OF 30A   Lucky Dog. 2010

Retired Racer
ADOPTED FROM
A WISCONSIN RESCUE
ORGANIZATION

"Grayson has led us even closer to humanity than what we could have ever conceived!"

Grayson
Santa Rosa Beach at Gulf Place
Loved by: Alice & David McClary

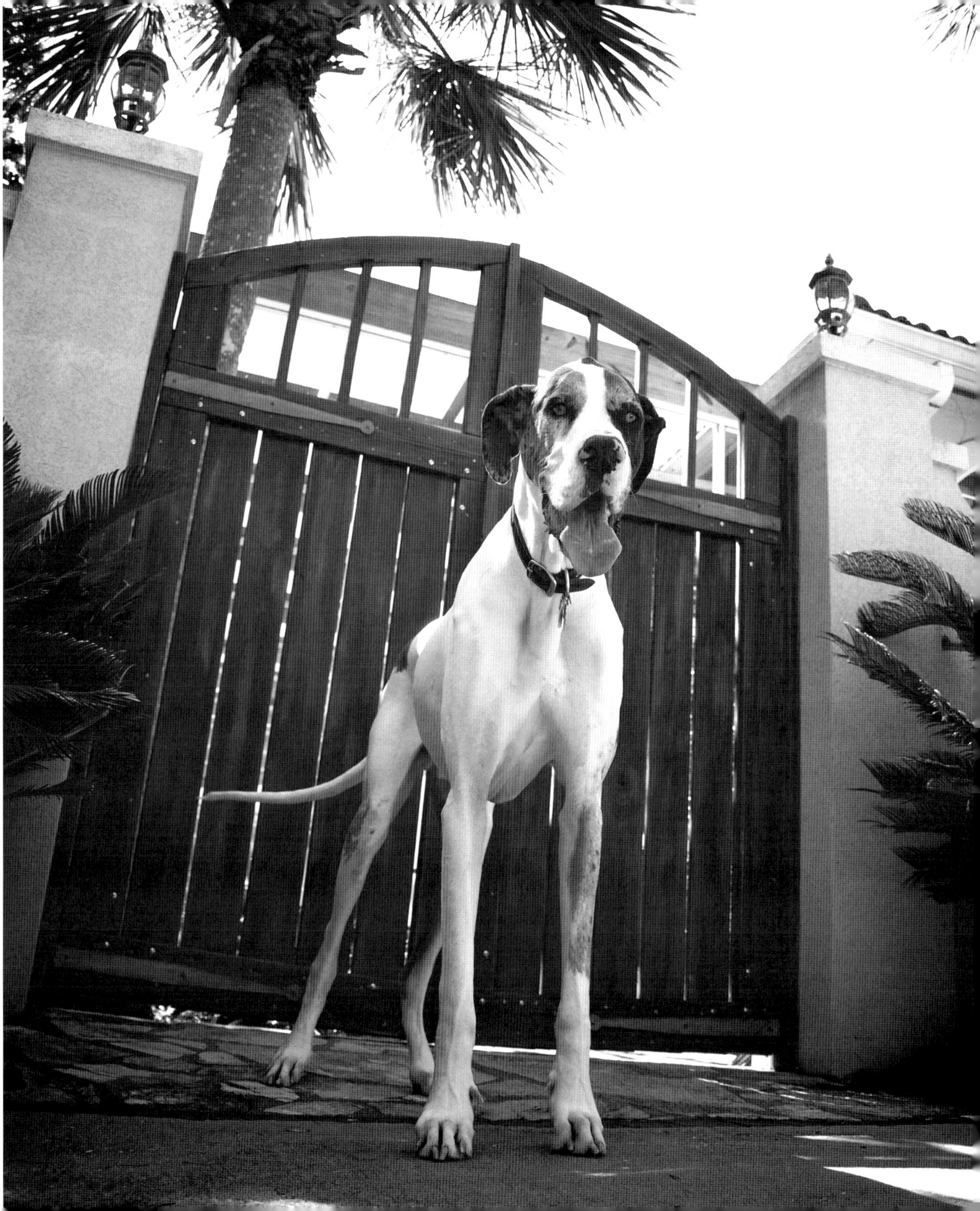

RESCUED
Adopted from
Chippewa County Humane
Association in Chippewa Falls, WI

Ellie
CERULEAN PARK
WATERCOLOR
LOVED BY: WENDY & KURT RUUD

RESCUED
ADOPTED FROM
COCKER SPANIEL RESCUE OF GEORGIA

Winston

CERULEAN PARK
WATERCOLOR
LOVED BY: WENDY & KURT RUUD

RESCUED
ADOPTED FROM SOUTHERN
HOPE HUMANE ASSOCIATION

Henry

CERULEAN PARK
WATERCOLOR
LOVED BY: WENDY & KURT RUUD

"Most of the dogs rescued from the puppy mill had never had chewy toys, treats, or human interaction. These days Henry, aka 'Happy Henry' is loving life in Florida... he and Winston enjoy their Saturday and Sunday morning car ride to McDonald's for our coffee, and their hash browns!"

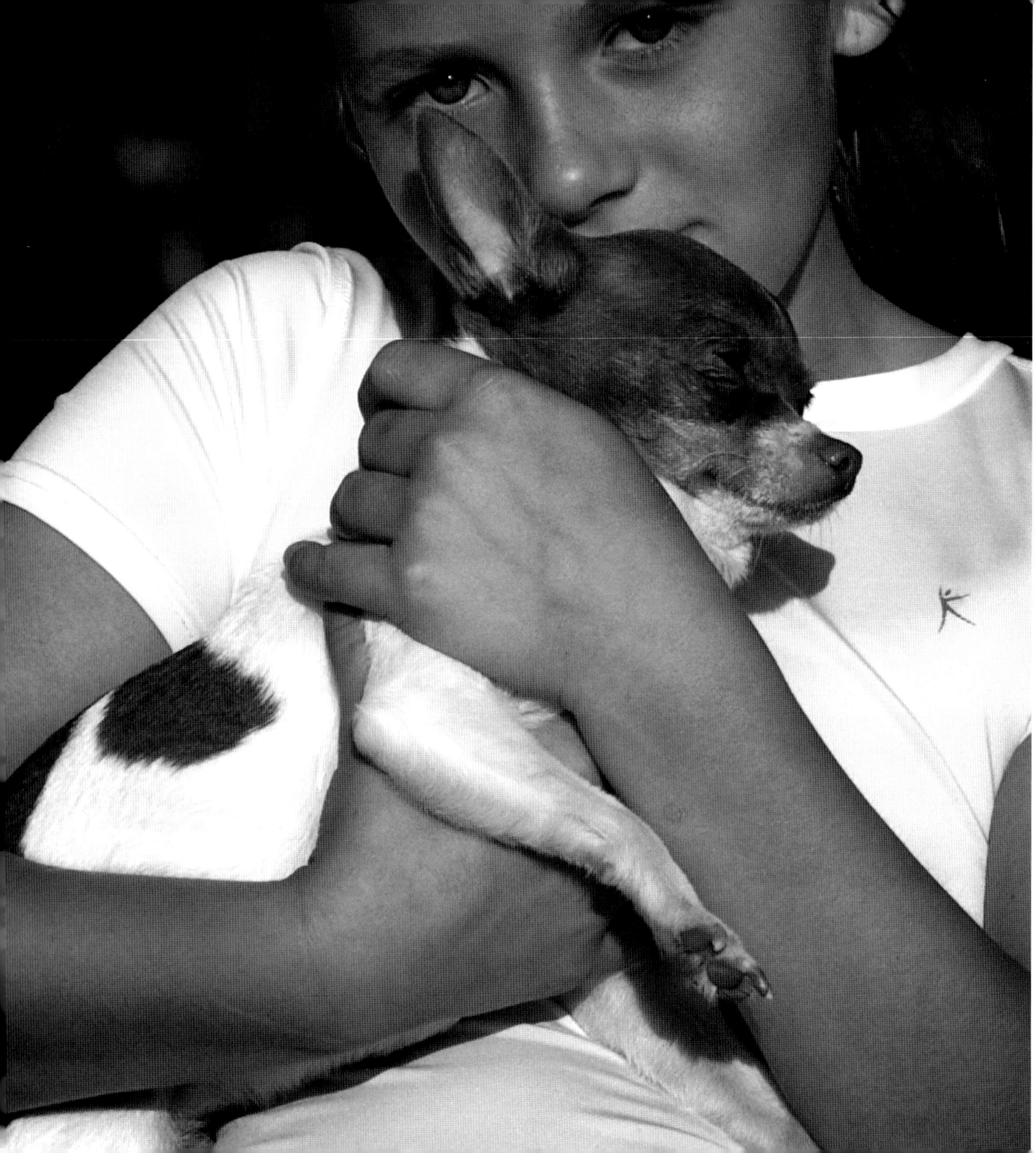

Sweet Pea
Choctawhatchee Bay
Loved by: The Flanagan Family

Harley
Choctawhatchee Bay
Loved by: The Flanagan & McCormick Family

Lady

Choctawhatchee Bay
Loved by: Gaye Farmer

Kodee

CHOCTAWHATCHEE BAY
LOVED BY: THE MCCORMICK FAMILY

Lucky Dog. 2010 THE DOGS OF 30A 171

Max

Jolee Island/Mermaid's Boutique
Sandestin
loved by: The Brundage Family

Holly Mae & Lola
SEACREST
LOVED BY: LEIGH VANDERELS

Wyatt

ROSEMARY BEACH
LOVED BY: FRAN & MICHAEL DAVINO

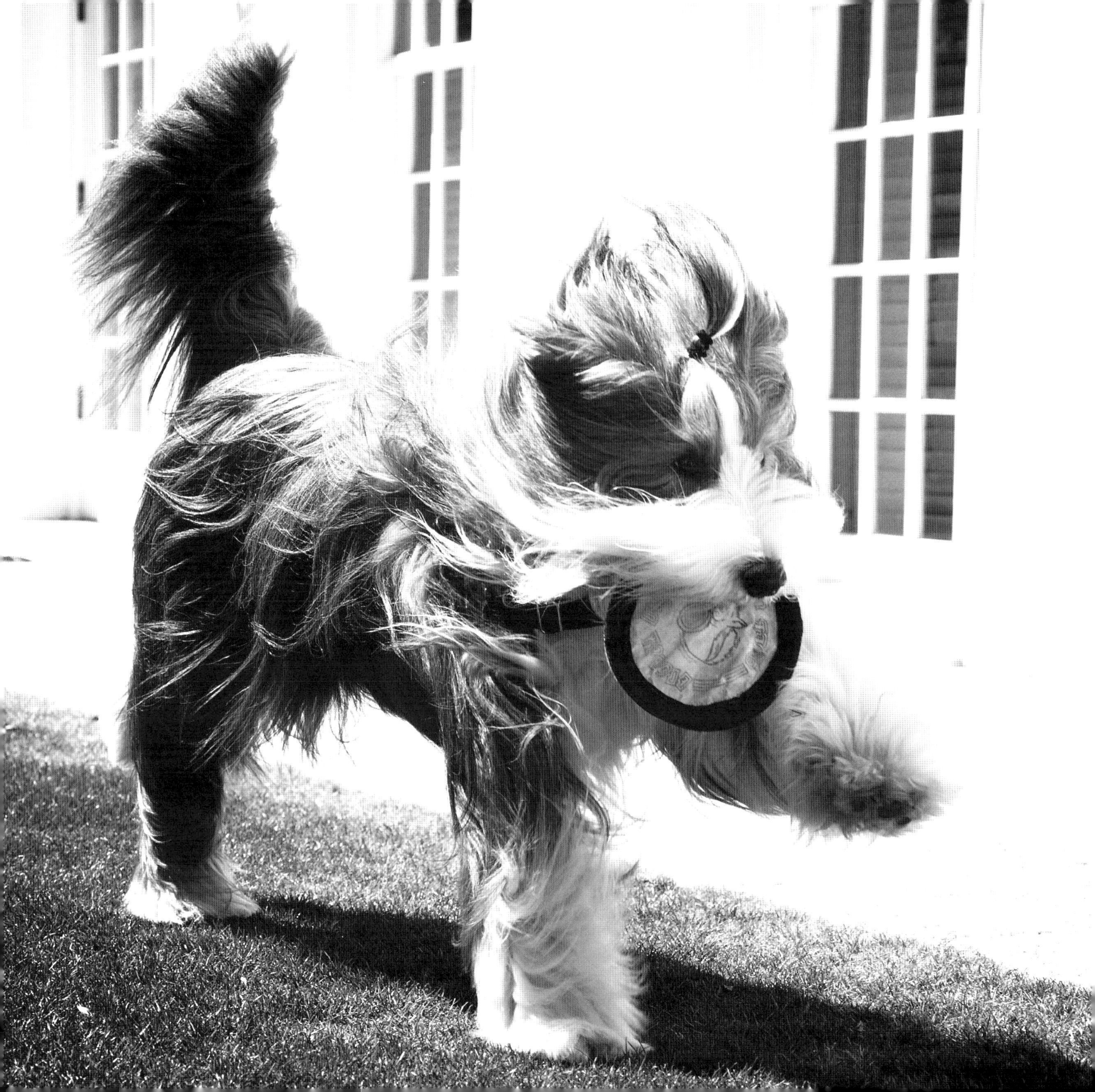

Gabby
SANDESTIN
LOVED BY: JOE & BETTE BUTLER

"I thought barking at doorbells was a bad thing, but not any more... it is my 'ace in the hole' to find Gabby when she has found a favorable spot and doesn't want to be disturbed!"

Bentley
Sandestin
Loved by: Caleb & Kristin Midgett

Roxy
SANDESTIN
LOVED BY: CALEB & KRISTIN MIDGETT

"Rusty had a really wonderful life. He did everything he ever wanted to do, has been places and seen things most dogs never get the chance to experience. We will never forget him."

~ In Loving Memory ~

Rusty
SANDESTIN
LOVED BY: TIM & GERRY MIDGETT

Destin

Sandestin
Loved by: Cheri Perry

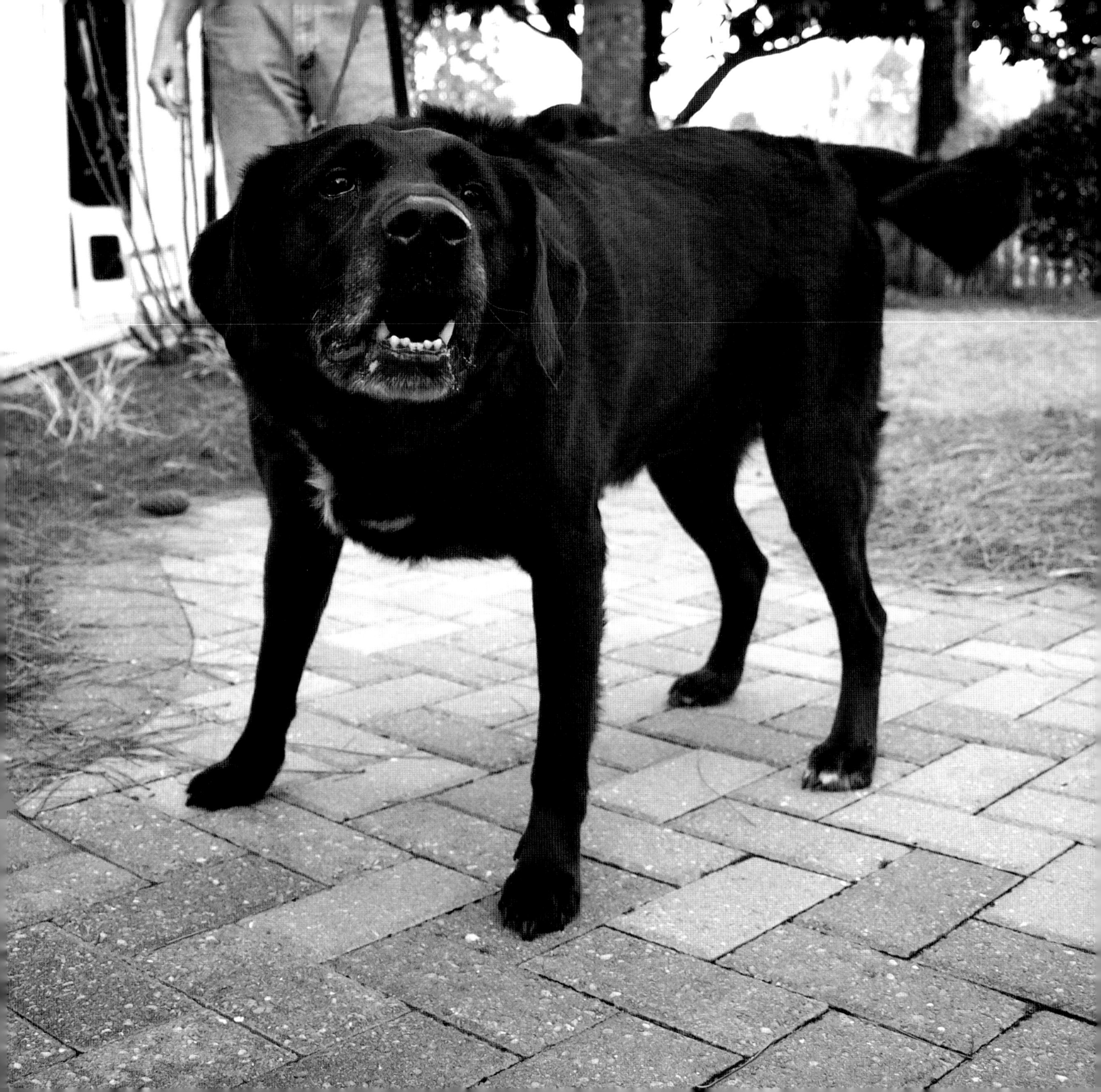

Coal
SANDESTIN
LOVED BY: CHIP & KELLY THOMAS

Angel
SANDESTIN
LOVED BY: CHIP & KELLY THOMAS

Princess Sophie Chica Pooch

SANDESTIN
LOVED BY: JESSICA HICKS

Molly

SANDESTIN
LOVED BY: DON & LAURA HILL

"When I called about the puppy, the owner said the chocolate male lab pup had already been purchased, but the little black female was still there, and they were taking her to the pound in the morning. One of the horrors I had recently learned about was something called 'Black Dog Syndrome,' which is a problem where black dogs are the most difficult to adopt, and are euthanized more than any other dog at the shelters. I just could not let this happen to this little girl. So now I am a three-dog (all black) household, and the pandemonium is crazy, but wonderful! It would not be home without them!"

Tully, Katy & Maddie

Teresa Cline Gallery
Grayton Beach
loved by: Teresa Cline

Lucky Dog. 2010

Lumpy
LUMPY'S WINE BAR
BAYTOWNE WHARF
LOVED BY: MIKE & DEE LEA

THE DOGS OF 30A Lucky Dog. 2010

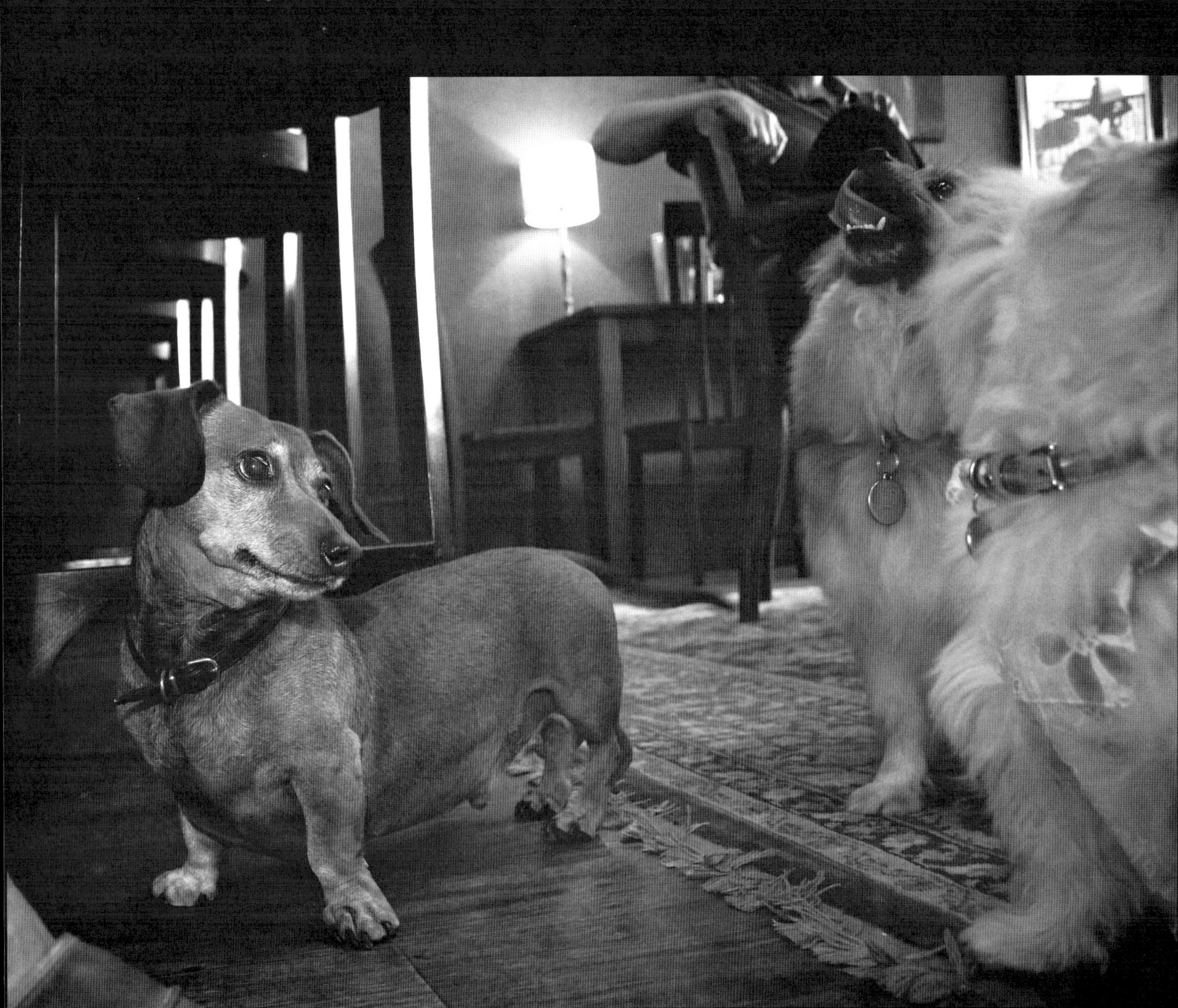

RESCUED
Adopted from PAWS, Ft. Walton Beach, Florida

"She is the best friend I could have ever asked for."

Sadie

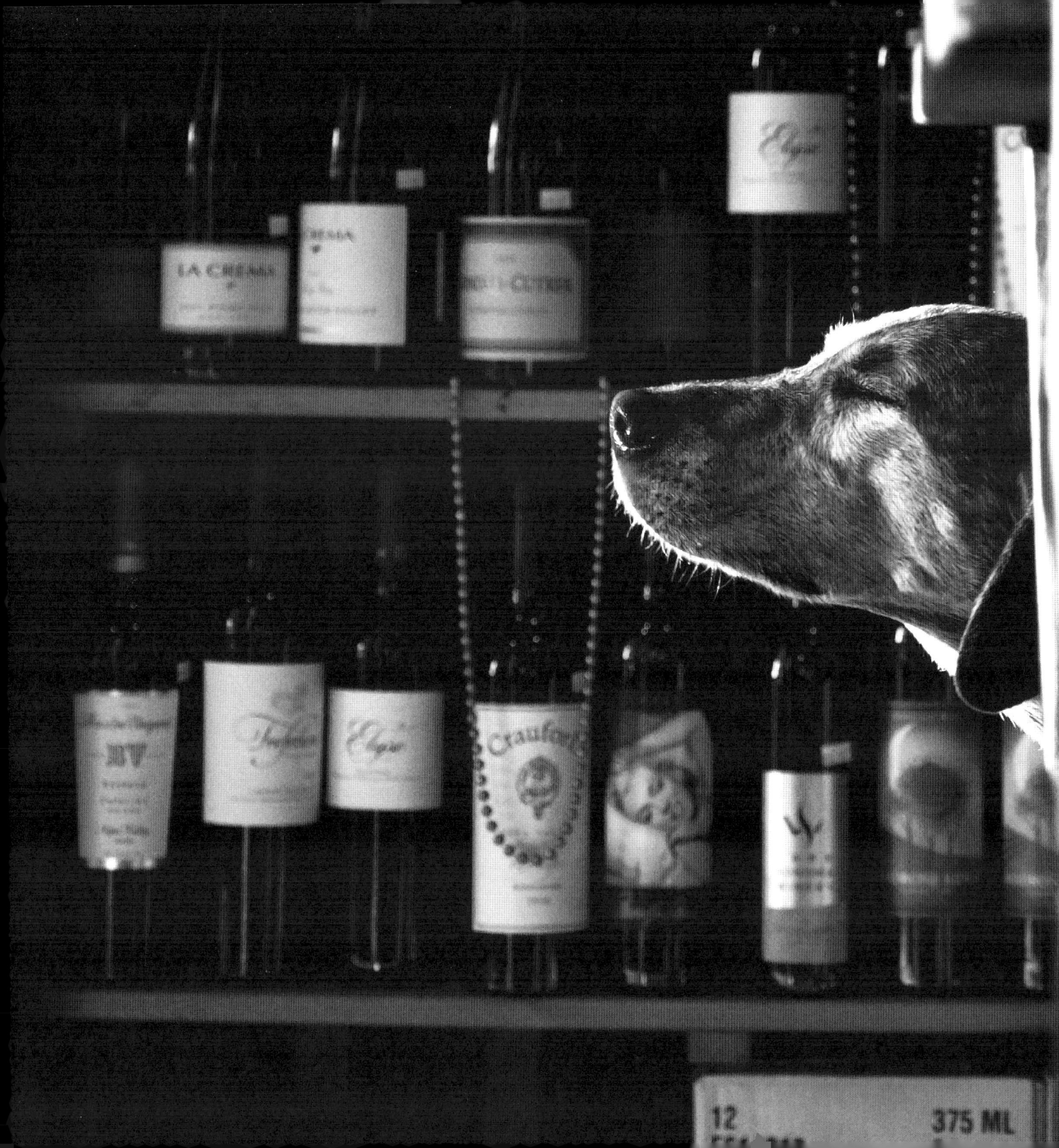
LA CREMA
12
375 ML

Bentley
LUMPY'S WINE BAR
BAYTOWNE WHARF
LOVED BY: DARLENE & LANCE GREENWALD

Hoot
LUMPY'S WINE BAR
BAYTOWNE WHARF
LOVED BY: DARLENE & LANCE GREENWALD

Sydney
Lumpy's Wine Bar
Baytowne Wharf
Loved by: Nancy Brown

Lucky Dog. 2010

Beany

Bubba

Beatrice

Lily

Bailey

Lumpy's Wine Bar
Baytowne Wharf
Loved by: Russell & Ann Shields

Blue

Lumpy's Wine Bar
Baytowne Wharf
Loved by: Hope & Christman Morgan

Looie, Lucy & Puppies
Seacrest Sundries
Seacrest
loved by: Larry & Beje Beasley

Zoe
LA CREMA
ROSEMARY BEACH
LOVED BY: RICK & JAN HELFAND

Gabby
ROSEMARY BEACH
LOVED BY: RICK & JAN HELFAND

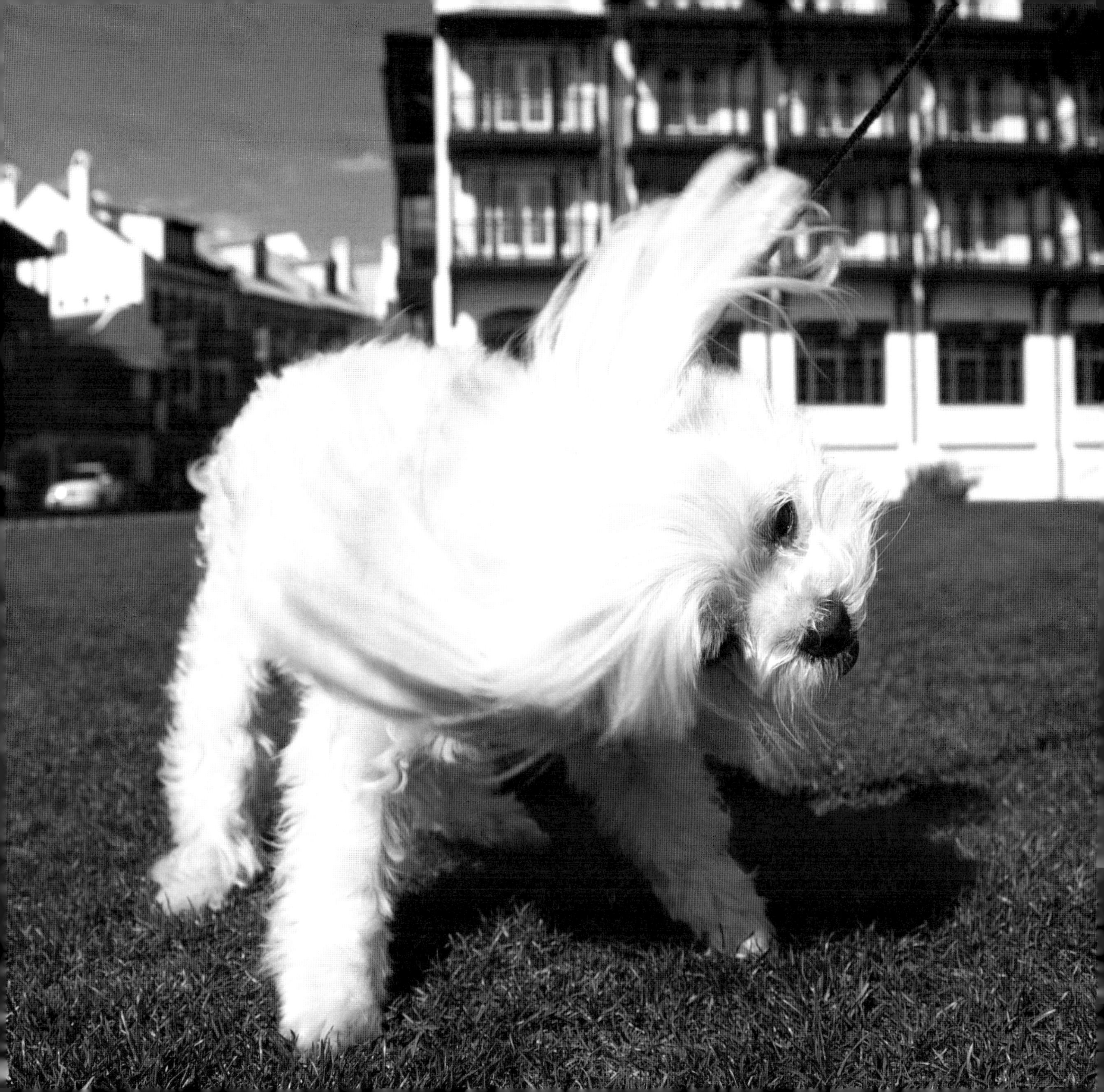

"We feel privileged to have him."

Woody
Great Southern Cafe
Seaside
Loved by: Tom & Dottie Hidell

RESCUED
ADOPTED FROM
RUFF

"Crusty's mother, and six other puppies were found under a bridge in Fort Walton and taken to RUFF. He is the only living survivor. When we first adopted him, he was afraid of everything, but, over the years, with patience and love, he has become the wonderful dog he is today."

Crusty

GREAT SOUTHERN CAFE
SEASIDE

LOVED BY: THOMAS & LEAH GOODSON

"Since my wife had already selected the time, the breed, the kennel, the gender... and then the specific puppy, all I wanted was to name our new addition. She agreed. While I was still mulling it over, my wife 'learned' (from a psychic) what name our new puppy (supposedly reincarnated from our previous dog) wanted to be called in her 'new life.' I made a list of the eight names I liked and left it for my wife to see. The first name on my list was 'Astrid.' Guess what? That's the name the psychic said she wanted to be called. End of story."

Oscar & Chester

Rosemary Beach

Loved by: Jessica Duggan

Astrid

Rosemary Beach

Loved by: Julie & Lee Wilcox

G-Dog
LA VIE EST BELLE
SEASIDE
LOVED BY: AIMEE ALDERSON & EVERYONE AT LA VIE EST BELLE

"I wish I could say that I rescued G-Dog, but he actually rescued me."

RESCUED
ADOPTED FROM PAWS
LYNNWOOD, WASHINGTON

"From the shy pup at the pound, Arthur has become an avid traveller and adventure-seeker. Weather permitting, he can be spotted flanked by five Rhodesian Ridgebacks trotting along with horses on a long trail ride through the mountains."

Arthur
SEASIDE
LOVED BY: CRISTINA PODLUSKY

Lucky Dog. 2010   THE DOGS OF 30A   205

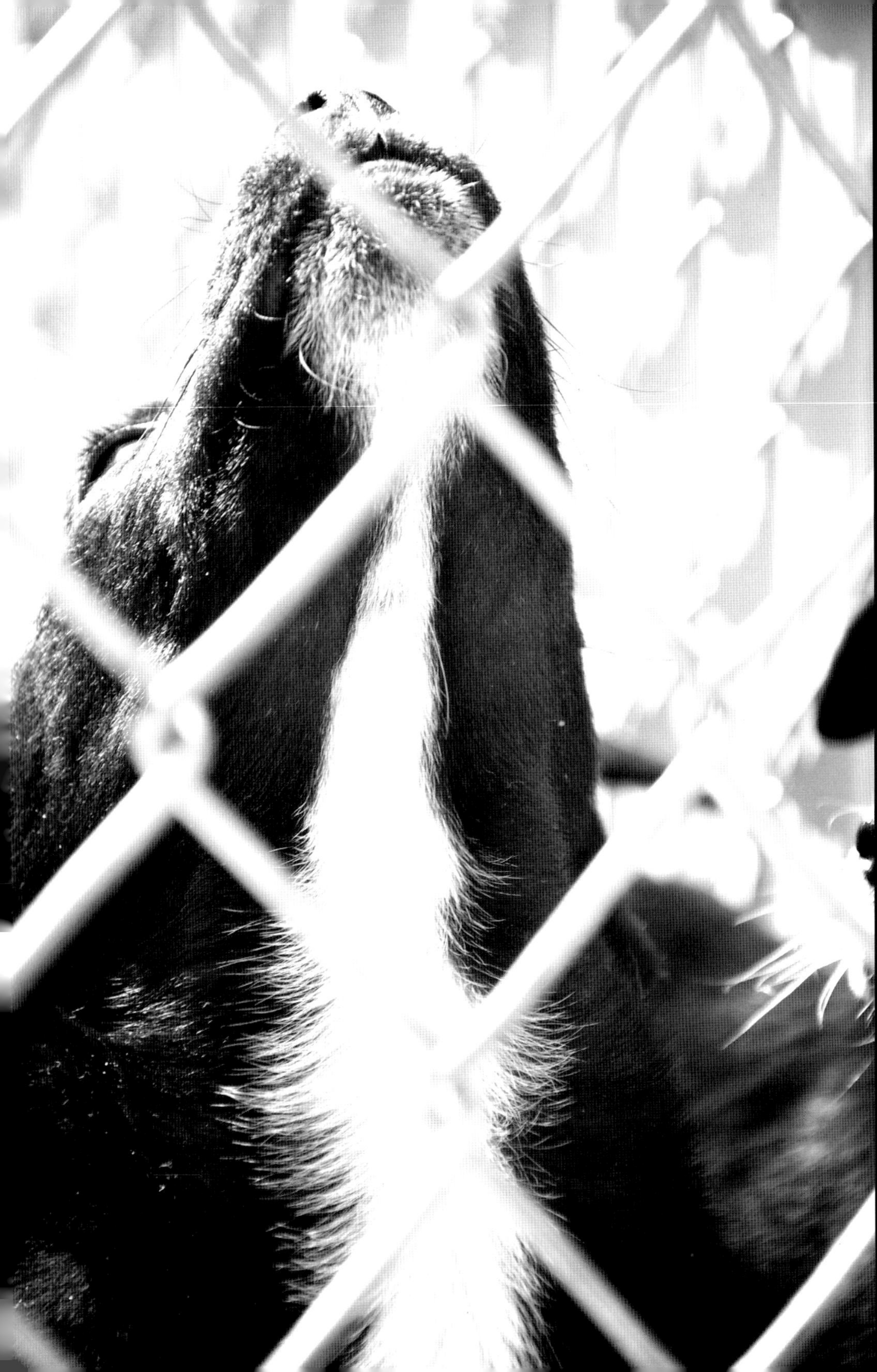
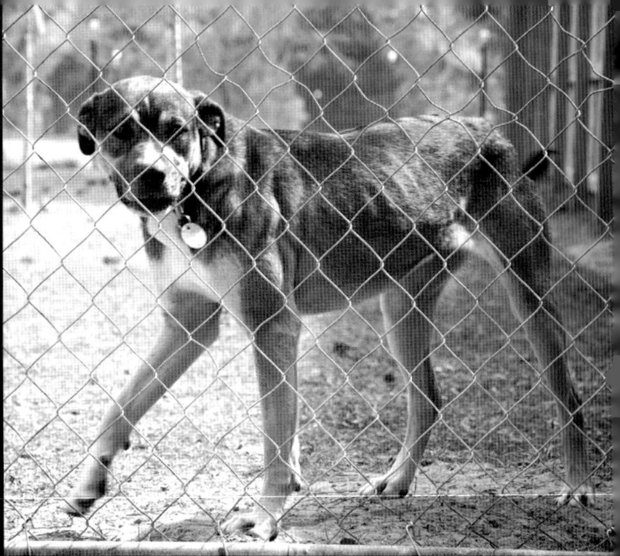
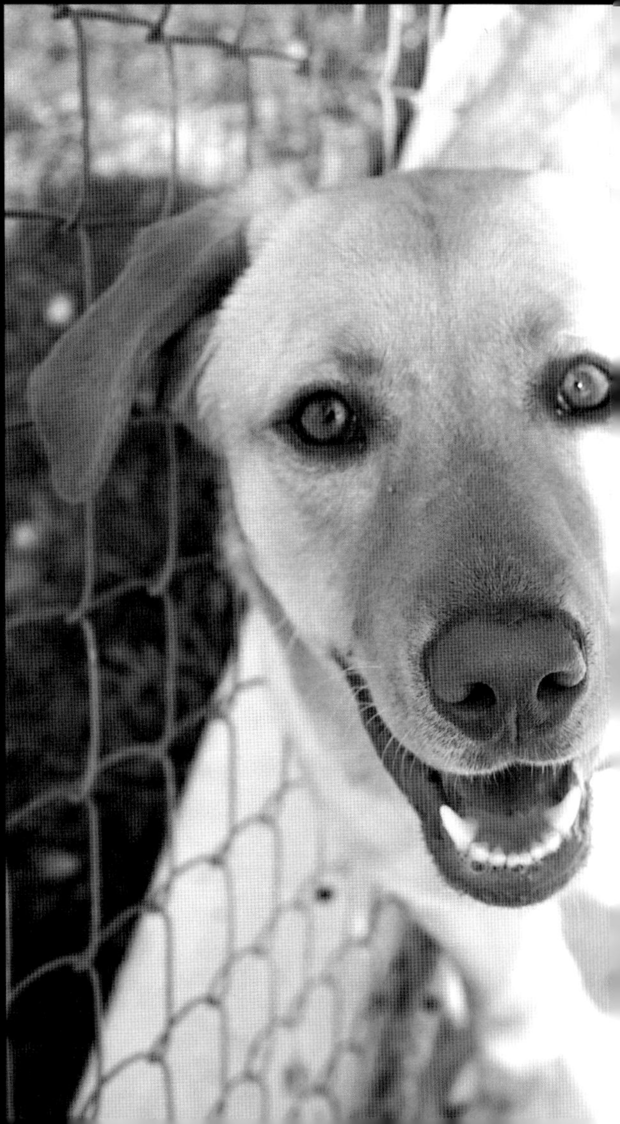

A portion of the proceeds of this book will be donated to Alaqua.

DEDICATION
This Book is Dedicated to the Alaqua Animal Refuge

ALAQUA ANIMAL REFUGE, an independent, non-profit organization located on Florida's Emerald Coast, advocates the general welfare and humane treatment of animals by providing shelter, adoption services, and prevention of pet overpopulation. Located down a winding gravel road on a picturesque, ten-acre farm near the Choctawhatchee Bay in Freeport, Florida, Alaqua provides a haven for wayward animals of all types. Once homeless, lost, and abused, these animals now run and play in sun-soaked pastures, swim in cool ponds, relax on breezy screened porches, and graze in lush, green fields. These animals (over two hundred at any given time) have found safety and care at Alaqua, a unique, full-service, **no-kill shelter.**

Funded by grants, Alaqua recently made several improvements to the facility: renovations were made to an existing barn, a new barn was added in addition to two new quarantine buildings, two new infirmary buildings, six dog buildings, and two cat buildings.

Moving forward, Alaqua Animal Refuge is positioned to expand its services to include additional educational and community services through significant and innovative outreach programs. As Alaqua grows and develops, they are committed to their guiding purpose:

To Give Neglected, Lost and Abandoned Animals
A Chance at Life.

WWW.AARFLORIDA.COM

Design360, llc.

2117 Olde Towne Ave

Miramar Beach, FL 32550

http://www.design-360.com

Copyright "The Dogs of 30A" 2010

Photographer: Dr. Tonia Shatzel

Designer: Keri Atchley

Library of Congress Control Number: 2010929386

ISBN: 978-0-9845481-0-1

All rights reserved. No part of the publication may be reproduced, stored in or introduced into a retrieval system, or transmitted, in any form or by any means (electronic, mechanical, photocopying, recording, or otherwise), without the prior written permission of both the copyright owner and the above publisher of the book.

The scanning, uploading, and distribution of this book via the Internet or via any other means without the permission of the publisher is illegal and punishable by law. Your support of the photographer's and designer's rights is appreciated.